Right to Education
and
Revitalizing Education

J.C. Aggarwal
S. Gupta

SHIPRA

(First Published in 2010)

Rs. 800, US$ 40

ISBN: 978-81-7541-827-1

2016 Impression

Right to Education and Revitalizing Education

Published by:

SHIPRA PUBLICATIONS
LG 18-19, Pankaj Central Market,
I.P. Ext., Patparganj, Delhi 110092, India
Ph.: +91 11 22235152/6152
Email: info@shiprapublication.com
Website: www.shiprapublication.com

Preface
The Inconvenient Truth

The authors of the book are acutely aware of the fact that their views contained in the book are likely to raise many eyebrows and may receive severe criticism and brickbats at the hands of some sections working in the field of education on account of the exposure of their inadequacies.

For the last about five decades the planning, management and monitoring of education have been in the hands of the technocrats (IAS, PCS, etc.) and armchair academicians working in National and State level educational institutes. Despite their best efforts, the provisions of the Article 45 of the Constitution which envisaged the target of universal free and compulsory elementary education by 1960 is still elusive. This shows the lacunae in the field of education. A perusal of the history of educational reforms in India clearly indicates that the educational practitioners have not been given due share in the formulation of educational policies and programmes. The state of education today could thus be attributed to the poor capability and quality of personnel assigned to frame and implement policies which were unrealistic in ambition, unachievable in scope and non-pragmatic in implementation. The gloom and malaise of the education system may continue unless the diagnosis is correct'.

This book is not based on the recommendations of high profile educationists but is written by grass-roots level practitioners who have practical experience of teaching, administration and supervision at various levels of school education. During the course of his thirty years of service of one the authors has interacted with thousands of school teachers and is alive to their views on what ails the present education policies and programmes.

The book presents some practical but unconventional recommendations regarding education reforms. However, these do not involve substantial financial implications.

The first and the foremost premise of 'Education Reforms' is to provide adequate teaching staff, infrastructure and teaching-learning material. At the same time it must be ensured that the teachers teach effectively and the students understand to learn economically and efficiently.

The authors are grateful to the publishers and the authors whose publications they have consulted in preparing this work.

26 January, 2010

J.C. Aggarwal
S. Gupta

Contents

1

A Brief History of Education Reforms in India

The first important effort for reforms in education in India was made by Mahatma Gandhi. Gandhiji emphasised that primary education should be imparted through a craft and should be self-supporting, 'I want that the whole process of education to be imparted through some craft.'

Gandhiji's views were considered and given a concrete shape in October 1937 in a Conference of National Workers at Wardha. The Conference appointed a Committee of distinguished educationists under the chairmanship of Dr. Zakir Hussain to prepare a detailed scheme. The report of the Committee published in March 1938, came to be known as Wardha Scheme of Education. It was approved by Gandhiji and was placed before the Indian National Congress at its Haripura session held in March 1938. The Congress accepted the scheme. The scheme has three important features: (1) Free and compulsory education for seven years on a nationwide scale; (2) Mother tongue to be the medium of instruction; and (3) Education to centre around some form of manual and productive work with due regard to the environment of the child.

The Basic System of Education or the Wardha Scheme of Education or the *Nai Talim* was accepted as the national system of education at the school stage, at the dawn of Independence. After the publication of the Report of the Education Commission 1964-66, the scheme went into oblivion. Many protagonists of this scheme described the report as the 'Deathknell of Basic Education'.

After independence the first action of a great significance in the field of education taken by the Government of India was the appointment of the University Education Commission in December 1948, under the Chairmanship of Dr. S. Radhakrishnan, an eminent scholar and former Vice-Chancellor of Banaras University, who later on became the second President of India. The Commission submitted its report in August 1949. The report of the Commission is an unique document of importance as it guided the development of university education in India till the formation of the National Policy on Education, 1968. While outlining the aims of university education, the Commission said, 'The greatness of a country does not depend on the extent of its territory, the length of its communications or the amount of wealth, not even on widespread education or equitable distribution of wealth, important as all these things are. If we wish to bring about a savage upheaval in our society, a *raksasa raj*, all that we need to do is to give vocational and technical education and starve the spirit. We will have a number of scientists without conscience, technicians, without taste who finds a void within themselves, a moral vacuum and a desperate need to substitute something, anything, for their lost endeavour and purpose. Society will then get what it deserves. If we claim to be civilised we must develop thought for the poor and the suffering chivalrous regard and respect for women, faith on human brotherhood regardless of race or colour, nation or religion, love of peace and freedom, abhorrence of cruelty and ceaseless devotion of the claims of justice.'

The second most significant document in the history of the development of education is the Report of the Secondary Education Commission 1952-53.

Writing about the aims of the secondary education in accordance with the needs of democratic India, the Commission observed, '...we shall have to formulate our aims with reference to these broad categories—the training of character to fit the students to participate creatively as citizens in the emerging democratic social order; the improvement of their practical and vocational efficiency so that they may play their part in building up the economic prosperity of their country, and the development of their literary artistic and cultural interests, which are necessary for self-expression and for the full development of the human personality, without which a living national culture cannot come into being.' The recommendation of the Commission, unfortunately remained unfulfilled by and large.

In 1966, an important event in the history of education in India took place. This was the publication of the report of the Education Commission 1964-66, popularly known as the Kothari Commission after the name of its Chairman D.S. Kothari. The report went into all aspects of education and at all levels and suggested a blueprint of educational reforms to be carried out during the coming twenty years. The report appropriately subtitled *Education and National Development* begins with these words, 'The destiny of India is now being shaped in our classrooms. This, we believe, is no more rhetoric. In a world based on science and technology, it is education that determines the level of prosperity, welfare and security of the people.' It concludes with these remarks, 'We must either build a sound, balanced, effective and imagined educational system to meet our developing needs and respond to challenging aspirations or be content to be swept aside by the strong currents of history.'

The Commission identified the three important facets of the big programme that would bring about the desired 'educational revolutions'—

- internal transformation so as to relate it to the life, needs and aspirations of the nation;
- qualitative improvement so that the standards achieved are adequate, keep continually rising, and at least in a few sectors become internationally comparable; and
- expansion of educational facilities broadly on the basis of manpower needs and with an accent on equalization of educational opportunities.

For the internal transformation of the system of education the following programmes urged high priority.

(1) Work experience as an integral part of general education;

vocationalisation of education at the secondary level; improvement of professional education and research, promoting national consciousness;

(2) Introducing a common school system, making social and national service compulsory; developing all modern Indian languages;

(3) making science education an integral part of all school education and developing scientific research; and

(4) Inculcation of high values—social, moral and spiritual- at all stages of education.

The Report received wide attention and aroused great hopes. Its recommendations had been the major base for the declaration of the National Policy on Education (1968); and the Fourth, Fifth and Sixth Five-Year Plans. More than four decades have passed since the publication of the Report and yet many of its significant recommendations especially on vocationalisation of secondary education, common school system and educational planning on manpower needs have not been implemented.

The Commission recommended that the Government of India should issue a statement on the National Policy on Education which should provide guidelines to the State Governments and the local authorities in preparing and implementing educational plans in their areas. Therefore, in 1967, the Government of India constituted the Committee of members of Parliament on Education to prepare the draft of a statement on the National Policy on Education. Dr. Triguna Sen, the Union Education Minister was the chairman of the Committee which included 29 leading members of all the different political parties in the country. A Drafting Committee under the chairmanship of Shri Ganga Saran was constituted from among the members of the Committee. The Committee arrived 'at the greatest common measure of agreement' and evolved the draft of a National Policy on Education. It was placed before the Central Advisory Board of Education (CABE) which met in 1967 and discussed the formulation of a National Policy. During the discussion it was realized that the policy should be as brief as possible and should define clearly and realistically the new directions of the changes proposed for education at all levels in the country. A general consensus emerged in the course of the Board's deliberations. Thereafter the Government of India passed the issued National Policy on Education (1968). The Resolution inter alia states, 'The Government of India is convinced that a radical reconstruction of education on the broad lines recommended by the Education Commission is essential for economic and cultural development of the country for national integration and for realising the ideal of a socialistic pattern of society.' The Government of India accordingly resolved to promote the development of education in the country in accordance with seventeen principles.

About the educational structure, the policy statement said 'It will be advantageous to have a broadly uniform educational structure in all parts of the country. The ultimate objective should be to adopt the 10+2+3 pattern, the higher secondary stage of two years being located in schools, colleges or both according to local conditions.'

Resolution also envisaged that the Government of India would 'also review every five years 'the progress made and recommend guidelines for future development.'

In 1972, the Ministry of Education and Social Welfare appointed a committee consisting of 11 members to suggest practical steps to be taken for implementation of the pattern for the school and college classes in all States and Union Territories of the country and to estimate the cost of implementing the programme. The committee, headed by Dr. P.D. Shukla as Chairman and Dr. R.P. Singhal, Secretary, Central Board of Secondary Education as Member-Secretary, submitted its report in November 1973.

The Report of the Committee provided guidelines for the implementation of the new pattern of education.

In November 1974, the CABE adopted a resolution recommending the introduction of the 10 + 2 + 3 pattern of education all over the country during the Fifth Plan Period. By the end of 1976-77, this pattern had been introduced in 19 States and Union Territories. It has now been accepted in all parts of the country. According to the modified National

Policy on Education, 1992, efforts will be made to have the +2 stage accepted as a part of school education throughout the country.

With the coming of the Janata Government in power in 1977 at the Centre, the first question in the field of education to be raised was whether the Resolution on National Policy on Education (1968) should be reviewed. The new Government declared that it would review all educational programmes including the National Policy. The Government appointed the Ishwarbhai Patel Committee and the Adiseshiah Committee to review the educational programmes in classes I to X and classes XI to XII respectively. The University Grants Commission was also requested to review all its programmes. The draft of the revised National Policy on Education which the Government had promised to the people was released in 1979.

The New Pattern of Education 10 + 2 had been introduced in several schools of the country. The NCERT had prepared new curriculum and textbooks which came under heavy criticism and it was felt that the curriculum was overloaded. The Ishwarbhai Patel Review Committee scrutinised the scheme of studies and suggested some modifications. The Review Committee also defined the concept of Socially Useful Productive Work (SUPW). This, by and large, replaced the concept of Work Experience and Craft Based education.

The National Review Committee (1978-78) on Higher Secondary Education, headed by Dr. Malcolm S. Adiseshiah, Vice-Chancellor, Madras University, reviewed the NCERT's document 'Higher Secondary Education and its Vocationalisation' and recommended a plan of action for vocationalisation of education at the secondary/higher stage. The Report of the Committee is entitled 'Learning To Do-Towards a Learning and Working Society.'

The 1968 National Policy on Education had stipulated a review of progress every five years. Such a review was overdue. In the meanwhile there had been a change of Government at the Centre. The Janata Government, in pursuance of its election manifesto decided to frame a new national education and for this purpose a Draft National Policy on Education (1979) was issued. Since the Janata Dal Government was short-lived, the policy could not be finalised.

In 1985, the NCERT prepared a '*National Curriculum for Elementary and Secondary Education: A Framework.*' The document covered four broad areas—emerging concerns and imperatives, curriculum organisation, evaluation and implementation.

On becoming the Prime Minister, Shri Rajiv Gandhi, in his broadcast to the nation on January 1, 1985, declared that a new education policy to 'equip the country both scientifically and economically to enter the 21st century' would be formulated soon. Accordingly, the Ministry of Education, Government of India, prepared a document named *Challenge of Education—A Policy Perspective, 1985.*

The document, presented to the Prime Minister and the Parliament in August 1985, contained an overview of the state of education in the country, pointed out the directions of future initiatives based essentially on the views and suggestions from educational planners, teachers, students, parents, intellectuals and citizens interested in education. It aimed at providing the basis for a nationwide debate for facilitating the formulation of the new education policy. It also formed the basis of discussions in the conference of State Ministers of Education, held on August 29-30, 1985. It was translated practically into all regional languages of the country and given wide circulation. In addition, 5,80,000 copies of the document in English, 2,40,000 in Hindi and 4,000 in Urdu were distributed by the Ministry in response to requests received from and also to different organisations. As a part of the nationwide debate, 12 National Seminars and 17 Sponsored Seminars were organised by the Government of India and its agencies.

More than 8,000 communications were received by the Ministry of Education. In 1986, the Ministry of Education, now renamed the Ministry of Human Resource Development, Government of India, brought out a revised document *National Policy on Education, 1986—A Presentation* which was discussed in meetings of the State Minister of Education, the National Development Council and the Central Advisory Board of Education. The document was again revised in the light of discussions and the *Draft National Policy on Education 1986* was placed on the table of Parliament in the first week of May, 1986. The draft was debated and finally adopted by the Lok Sabha on May 8 and Rajya Sabha on May 12, 1986. Thus the National Policy on Education, 1986 emerged.

The National Policy on Education (NPE) 1986 marks a significant step in the history of education in post Independent India. It contains XII parts and 157 Paragraphs (i) Introductory; (ii) The Essence and Role of Education; (iii) National System of Education; (iv) Education for Duality; (v) Reorganisation of Education at Different Stages; (vi) Technical and Management of Education; (vii) Making the System Work; (viii) Re-orienting the Content and Process of Education; (ix) The Teacher; (x) The Management of Education, (xi) Resources and Review; and (xii) The Future.

With a view to implementing the NPE, the Ministry of Human Resource Development undertook an extensive exercise to prepare a programme of Action. Twenty-three Task Forces were constituted and each was assigned a specific subject covered by the NPE. The Task Forces submitted their reports in July 1986. These reports were discussed in a series of meetings taken by the Minister of Human Resource Development. After these discussions were completed, a conference of Education Secretaries of the State Governments and Union Territories Administrators was convened on 20 July, 1986. Suggestions received during this meeting were considered and the Programme of Action was prepared with reference to the main areas covered in NPE. The CABE met at New Delhi on August 1 and 2, 1986.

The document on the Programme of Action was discussed at this meeting. The final Programme of Action was presented to Parliament on August 8, 1986. The Lok Sabha and the Rajya Sabha discussed and approved the Programme of Action on August 22 and 23, 1986 respectively. It was the first time in the history of independent India that a National Policy on Education was prepared at the initiative of a Prime Minister and that a Programme of Action was planned for bringing about educational reforms.

Among the most important programmes initiated at the school stages are: Blackboard Operation at the primary stage, Pace-Setting of Navodaya Vidyalayas and the Vocationalisation of Education at the secondary stage. In the field of Teacher Education, District Institutes of Education and Training have been set up and selected Secondary Teacher Education Institutions upgraded into Colleges of Teacher Education/Institutions of Advanced Study in Education (CTEs/IASEs).

In the field of Higher Education, some of the major thrust areas are: Strengthening Autonomous Colleges, Redesigning Courses, Academic Staff Colleges for Orientation of Teachers and Eligibility Tests for Recruitment of Lecturers etc.

In 1988, NCERT developed syllabi at the school stage. In this context it is hardly necessary to stress that a detailed syllabi form an important link in the process of curriculum development. The new syllabi were meant for serving as an effective instrument for initiating the desired educational goals. The syllabi were finalised in a national level meeting attended by representatives of State Boards of School/Secondary Education, Kendriya Vidyalaya Sangathan and SCERTs/SIEs.

With a view to implementing the directions contained in the National Policy on Education, 1986 regarding 'Reorienting the Content and Process of Education', the NCERT revised the curriculum in 1988. The revised curriculum was the outcome of the deliberations of a large member of seminars participated by eminent educationists, curriculum specialists, subject experts, principals of schools, teacher educators, legislators, journalists and representatives of teachers organisations. The publication incoporates in it emerging concerns and imperatives, curriculum concerns, basis for the national system of education, factors related to the organisation of the curriculum, allocation of time to different areas, evaluation and examination etc. It also suggests the strategy of implementation.

Two reports on teachers also deserve attention in the context of educational reforms in India. For the first time two

National Commissions on Teachers were appointed by the Government of India in 1983. The reports though submitted in 1985 and published in 1986 were made public only in 1987. It is sad to note that these reports received little attention of the concerned authorities.

Of course, the recommendations of the Commission on School Teachers regarding the pay scales have led to agitations by the teachers. Mention may be made of the two important observations made by the Commission on Teachers. The Commissions on School Teachers concludes Chapter II with these words, 'Status, by reason of a title or position will become increasingly difficult to come by, we feel. Status, in other words, will have to be earned by the teacher as any other professional worker....So must the new teacher earn status through achievement.' The other Commission concluded Chapter II by stating, 'The National Commission on Teachers in Higher Education would therefore make a fervent plea on the one hand to the Government to appreciate how potent the teacher is in engineering social change and hence to provide him status, encouragement and resources for the purpose and on the other to the teachers to open their minds and hearts to the new possibilities and to discharge their responsibilities with an urgent sense of social purpose.'

The political scenario has greatly affected the implementation of the NPE. In the November 1989 Lok Sabha poll, Rajiv's Congress Party lost and in December, the Janata Dal Government was formed with V.P. Singh as Prime Minister. The BJP and the Left Parties decided to give outside support to Janata/NF Government.

In pursuance of its election manifesto, the National Front Government appointed on May 7, 1990, a Committee with Acharya Ramamurti as its Chairman, to review the National Policy on Education (NPE), 1986. The Committee submitted its report to the Minister of State in the Ministry of Human Resource Development on December 26, 1990. The report was tabled in Parliament on January 9, 1991. During this period political changes of far reaching consequences took place. V.P. Singh's Government was voted out on November 7, 1990 and Chandra Shekhar became Prime Minister on November 10. Chandra Shekhar's Government lasted for a very brief period between November 10, 1990 to March 6, 1991. Thereafter he worked as a caretaker Prime Minister till June 20. Shri P.V. Narasimha Rao assumed office of the Prime Minister of India on June 21, 1991, after the victory of party in the polls. Under the changed situation, the Ramamurti Report could not receive government patronage.

The recommendations of the Ramamurti Review Committee Report were examined by the Janardhana Committee appointed by the Central Advisory Board of Education in July 1991. The Janardhana Committee submitted its recommendations in January 1992. The CABE considered the Janardhana Committee Report in the first week of May 1992 and finalised the revised NPE.

The Revised NPE was presented in both Houses of Parliament on May 7, 1992 by then Human Resource Development Minister Arjun Singh. Apart from tabling the Revised NPE, Shri Singh also presented the Report of the Janardhana Committee (Central Advisory Board of Education's Committee). In his statement, the Minister said 'the NPE, 1986 has stood the test of time and enunciated a comprehensive framework to guide the development of education'. He further observed that while that framework continues to be relevant, the development during the last few years and the experience in implementation of the policy have necessitated certain modifications.

In the field of higher education also, a number of committees have made recommendations for carrying out the directions contained in the NPE.

The NDA Government introduced the national curriculum framework for School Education 2002 which was implemented for about 4 years.

With the coming in power of the UPA, the NCERT prepared a national curriculum in the light of the report '*Learning without Burden 1993*'. A 35 member National Steering Committee was constituted under the chairmanship of Prof. Yash Pal, former chairman UGC. The National Curriculum was approved by the CABE in Sept. 2005.

The latest series of reforms were initiated by HRD Minister Kapil Sibal. In the meanwhile, two other reports—one by the Knowledge Commission 2005-06 and the Renovation and Rejuvenation of Higher Education 2008-09 were published.

2

Sarva Shiksha Abhiyan

INTRODUCTION

Sarva Shiksha Abhiyan (SSA) is Government of India's flagship programme for achievement of Universalization of Elementary Education (UEE) in a time bound manner, as mandated by 86th amendment to the Constitution of India making free and compulsory Education to the Children of 6-14 years age group, a Fundamental Right.

SSA is being implemented in partnership with State Governments to cover the entire country and address the needs of 192 million children in 1.1 million habitations.

The programme seeks to open new schools in those habitations which do not have schooling facilities and strengthen existing school infrastructure through provision of additional class rooms, toilets, drinking water, maintenance grant and school improvement grants.

Existing schools with inadequate teacher strength are provided with additional teachers, while the capacity of existing teachers is being strengthened by extensive training, grants for developing teaching-learning materials and strengthening of the academic support structure at a cluster, block and district level.

SSA seeks to provide quality elementary education including life skills. SSA has a special focus on girl's education and children with special needs. SSA also seeks to provide computer education to bridge the digital divide.

The *Sarva Shiksha Abhiyan* programme is collectively supported by the World Bank, the European Commission and United Kingdom's DFID; of these the World Bank is the single largest contributor. In the first phase of support, between 2003 and 2006, the World Bank contributed $500 million of the total programme cost of $3.5 billion. World Bank lending for the programme is on confessional terms, with no interest and a repayment period of 35 years, with the first ten years as a "grace" period when no repayment is required.

Over 7,000 NGOs are participating in the SSA. They are helping to provide alternative education programmes or "bridge courses" to bring out-of-school children into the school system. They are also involved in monitoring the quality of education, capacity-building of Village Education Committees, and many function as reference groups advising States.

BASIC FEATURES OF SARVA SHIKSHA ABHIYAN

Introduction

Sarva Shiksha Abhiyan is an effort to universalise elementary education by community-ownership of the school system. It is in response to the demand for quality basic education all over the country. The SSA programme is also an attempt to provide an opportunity for improving human capabilities to all children, through provision of community-owned quality education in a Mission mode.

What is Sarva Shiksha Abhiyan?

- A programme with a clear **time frame** for universal elementary education.
- A response to the demand for **quality basic** education all over the country.
- An opportunity for promoting **social justice** through basic education.
- An effort at **effectively involving** the Panchayati Raj Institutions, School Management Committees, Village

and Urban Slum level Education Committees, Parents' Teachers' Associations, Mother Teacher Associations, Tribal Autonomous Councils and other grass root level structures in the management of elementary schools.

- An expression of **political will** for universal elementary education across the country.
- A **partnership** between the Central, State and the local government.
- An opportunity for States to develop their **own vision** of elementary education.

Aims of Sarva Shiksha Abhiyan

1. The Sarva Shiksha Abhiyan is to provide useful and relevant elementary education for all children in the 6 to 14 age group by 2010. There is also another goal to bridge social, regional and gender gaps, with the active participation of the community in the management of schools.
2. Useful and relevant education signifies a quest for an education system that is not alienating and that draws on community solidarity. Its aim is to allow children to learn about and master their natural environment in a manner that allows the fullest harnessing of their human potential both spiritually and materially. This quest must also be a process of value based learning that allow children an opportunity to work for each other's well being rather than to permit mere selfish pursuits.
3. Sarva Shiksha Abhiyan realizes the importance of Early Childhood Care and Education and looks at the 0-14 age as a continuum. All efforts to support pre-school learning in ICDS centres or special pre-school centres in non ICDS areas will be made to supplement the efforts being made by the ministry of Women and Child Development.

Mission Statement of Sarva Shiksha Abhiyan

1. The Sarva Shiksha Abhiyan Mission strives to secure the right to quality basic education for all children in the 6-14 years age group. The goals of the SSA Mission are:
   (a) Enrolment of all children in school, Education Guarantee Centre, Alternate school, 'Back-to-School' camp by 2005
   (b) Retention of all children till the upper primary stage by 2010
   (c) Bridging of gender and social category gaps in enrolment, retention and learning
   (d) Ensuring that there is significant enhancement in the learning achievement levels of children at the primary and upper primary stage.
2. Each State and district would set target dates by which the super goals of SSA would be achieved in their specific context, but not later than 2010.
3. National Norms would be developed for expected learning outcomes in certain essential skills. The progress towards enhancement in achievement levels on these norms would be assessed regularly on a sample basis at national level. In addition, States would evolve a mechanism for regular objective assessment of students' learning levels.
4. *The Mission Promotes:*
   (a) Empowering of children to be active participants in a knowledge society
   (b) A result oriented approach with accountability towards performance and output at all levels
   (c) A people centred mode of implementation of educational interventions with involvement of all stakeholders, especially teachers, parents, community and Panchayati Raj Institutions and voluntary organizations.
   (d) An equity based approach that focuses on the needs of educationally backward areas and disadvantaged social groups including children with special needs.
   (e) A holistic effort to ensure convergence of investments and initiatives for improving the efficiency of the elementary education system.
   (f) Institutional reforms and capacity building to ensure a sustained effort for UEE.

Why a Framework for Implementation (and not a Guideline)

1. (a) To allow States to formulate context specific guidelines within the overall framework
   (b) To encourage districts in States and UTs to reflect local specificity
   (c) To promote local need based planning based on broad National Policy norms
   (d) To make planning a realistic exercise by adopting broad national norms.
2. The objectives are expressed nationally though it is expected that various districts and States are likely to achieve universalization in their own respective contexts and in their own time frame. 2010 is the outer limit for such achievements. The emphasis is on mainstreaming out-of-school children through diverse strategies, as far as possible, and on providing eight years of schooling for all children in 6-14 age group. The thrust is on bridging of gender and social gaps and a total retention of all children in schools. Within this framework it is expected that the education system will be made relevant so that children and parents find the schooling system useful and absorbing, according to their natural and social environment.

Sarva Shiksha Abhiyan as a Framework and as a Programme

Sarva Shiksha Abhiyan (SSA) has two aspects:

(i) It provides a wide convergent framework for implementation of Elementary Education schemes.
(ii) It is also a programme with budget provision for strengthening vital areas to achieve universalization of elementary education.

While all investments in the elementary education sector from the State and the Central Plans will reflect as part of the SSA framework, they will all merge into the SSA programme within the next few years. As a programme, it reflects the additional resource provision for UEE.

Broad Strategies Central to SSA Programme

1. *Institutional Reforms*: As part of the SSA, the Central and the State governments will undertake reforms in order to **improve efficiency of the delivery system**. The States will have to make an objective assessment of their prevalent education system including educational administration, achievement levels in schools, financial issues, decentralisation and community ownership, review of State Education Act, rationalization of teacher deployment and recruitment of teachers, monitoring and evaluation, status of education of girls, SC/ST and disadvantaged groups, policy regarding private schools and ECCE. Many States have already carried out several changes to improve the delivery system for elementary education.

2. *Sustainable Financing*: The Sarva Shiksha Abhiyan is based on the premise that financing of elementary education interventions has to be **sustainable**. This calls for a long-term perspective on **financial partnership** between the Central and the State governments.

3. *Community Ownership*: The programme calls for community ownership of school-based interventions through **effective decentralisation**. This will be augmented by involvement of women's groups, VEC members and members of Panchayati Raj Institutions.

4. *Institutional Capacity Building*: The SSA conceives a major capacity building role for national, State and district level Institutions like NUEPA/NCERT/NCTE/SCERT/SIEMAT/DIET. **Improvement in quality** requires a sustainable support system of resource persons and institutions.

5. *Improving Mainstream Educational Administration*: It calls for **improvement of mainstream educational administration** by institutional development, infusion of new approaches and by adoption of cost effective and efficient methods.

6. *Community Based Monitoring with Full Transparency*: The Programme will have a community based monitoring system. **The Educational Management Information System (EMIS)** will correlate school level data with community-based information from micro planning and surveys. Besides this, every school will be encouraged to share all information with the community, including grants received. A notice board would be put up in every school for this purpose.

7. *Habitation as a Unit of Planning*: The SSA works on a **community based approach** to planning with habitation as a unit of planning. Habitation plans will be the basis for formulating district plans.

8. *Accountability to Community*: SSA envisages **cooperation** between teachers, parents and PRIs, as well as **accountability and transparency to the community**.

9. *Priority to Education of Girls*: Education of girls, especially those belonging to the scheduled castes and scheduled tribes and minorities, will be one of the **principal concerns** in Sarva Shiksha Abhiyan.

10. *Focus on Special Groups*: There will be a focus on the inclusion and participation of children from SC/ST, minority groups, urban deprived children, children of other disadvantaged groups and the children with special needs, in the educational process.

11. *Pre-Project Phase*: SSA will commence throughout the country with a well-planned pre-project phase that provides for a large number of interventions **for capacity development to improve the delivery and monitoring system**. These include provision for household surveys, community-based micro-planning and school mapping, training of community leaders, school level activities, support for setting up information system, office equipment, diagnostic studies, etc.

12. *Thrust on Quality*: SSA lays a special thrust on making education at the elementary level useful and relevant for children by improving the curriculum, child-centered activities and effective teaching learning strategies.

13. *Role of Teachers*: SSA recognizes the critical and central role of teachers and advocates a focus on their development

needs. Setting up of Block Resource Centres/Cluster Resource Centres, recruitment of qualified teachers, opportunities for teacher development through participation in curriculum-related material development, focus on classroom process and exposure visits for teachers are all designed to develop the human resource among teachers.

14. *District Elementary Education Plans*: As per the SSA framework, each district will prepare a District Elementary Education Plan reflecting all the investments being made and required in the elementary education sector, with a holistic and convergent approach. There will be a Perspective Plan that will give a framework of activities over a longer time frame to achieve UEE. There will also be an Annual Work Plan and Budget that will list the prioritized activities to be carried out in that year. The Perspective Plan will also be a dynamic document subject to constant improvement in the course of programme implementation.

Public-Private Partnership in SSA

Sarva Shiksha Abhiyan takes note of the fact that provision of elementary education is largely made by the government and government aided schools. There are also private unaided schools in many parts of the country that provide elementary education. Poorer households are not able to afford the fees charged in private schools in many parts of the country. There are also private schools that charge relatively modest fees and where poorer children are also attending. Some of these schools are marked by poor infrastructure and low paid teachers. Efforts will be made to explore areas of public private partnership. Government, Local Body, and government aided schools would be covered under the Sarva Shiksha Abhiyan, as is the practice under the Mid Day Meal scheme and DPEP. In case private sector wishes to improve the functioning of a government, local body or a private aided school, efforts to develop a partnership would be made within the broad parameters of State policy in this regard. Depending on the State policies, DIETs and other Government teacher-training institutes could be used to provide resource support to private unaided institutions, if the additional costs are to be met by these private bodies.

Financial Norms under Sarva Shiksha Abhiyan

1. The assistance under the programme of Sarva Shiksha Abhiyan will be on a 85:15 sharing arrangement during the IX Plan, 75:25 sharing arrangement during the X Plan for all States. During the XI Plan, it will be 65:35 for the first two years i.e. 2007-08 and 2008-09; 60:40 for the third year i.e. 2009-10; 55:45 for the fourth year i.e. 2010-11; and 50:50 thereafter i.e. from 2011-12 onwards between the Central Government and State Governments/Union Territories other than North Eastern States. For the 8 North-Eastern States, the fund sharing pattern between Centre and States shall be 90:10 under the programme during the XI Plan period and till the end of the programme with the Centre's share resourced from the 10 per cent earmarked funds for the North Eastern Region from the Central Budget for the SSA. (Ref. No. F.No. 2.40/2004-EE.3 dated 25th September, 2007) Commitments regarding sharing of costs would be taken from State governments in writing.
2. The State Governments will have to maintain their level of investment in elementary education as in 1999-2000. The contribution as State share for SSA will be over and above this investment.
3. The Government of India would release funds directly to the State Implementation Society. The further instalments would be released to the Society only after the State government has transferred its matching share to the society and expenditure of at least 50 per cent of the funds (Centre and States) transferred has been incurred.
4. The support for salary of teacher appointed under the SSA programme would be shared as per the funding pattern given in Para 19.1 above.

5. All legal agreements regarding externally assisted projects will continue to apply unless specific modifications have been agreed to, in consultation with foreign funding agencies.
6. Existing schemes of elementary education of the Department (except Mahila Samakhya, National Bal Bhawan and NCTE) will converge into SSA after the IX Plan. The National Programme for Nutritional Support to Primary Education (Mid-Day-Meal) would remain a distinct intervention.
7. District Education Plans would inter-alia, clearly show the funds/resources available for various components under schemes like PMGY, JGSY, PMRY, Sunishchit Rozgar Yojana, Area fund of MPs/MLAs, State Plan, foreign funding (if any) and resources generated in the NGO sector.
8. All funds to be used for upgradation, maintenance, repair of schools and Teaching Learning Equipment and local management to be transferred to VECs/ School Management Committees/ Gram Panchayat/or any other village/school level arrangement for decentralisation adopted by that particular State/UT. The village/school-based body may make a resolution regarding the best way of procurement.
9. Other incentive schemes like distribution of scholarships and uniform will continue to be funded under the State Plan. They will not be funded under the SSA programme.
10. The major financial norms under SSA

Source: Ministry of Human Resource Department. Department of Education Government of India.

3

The Rights of Children to Free and Compulsory Education Act, 2009 (35 of 2009): Elementary Education

BRIEF HISTORY OF LEGISLATION

When the Constitution of India was framed, there was no Article relating to Right to Education. Article 45 was introduced under Part IV **'Directive Principles of State Policy'.** The Article stated—**'Provision for free and compulsory education for children';** The state shall endeavour to provide within a period of ten years from the commencement of this Constitution, for free and compulsory education for all children until they complete the age of fourteen years'.

Vigorous efforts were made to implement the Article 45 but results were not satisfactory. From time to time great concerns were expressed in official and non-official circles on this. The target date of 1960 went on changing from year to year. The Government of India in 2001 initiated the Sarv Shiksha Abhiyan.

The Supreme Court of India while hearing a case pertaining to education advised the Government of India to enact a suitable Legislation for Universalization of Elementary Education (UEE). Accordingly the Constitution of India was amended by 'The Constitution (Eighty Sixth Amendment) Act 2002. The amendment included the following provisions:

(a) Insertion of new article 21A.—After article 21 of the constitution, the following article shall be inserted namely:

"21A. Right to Education.- The state shall provide free and compulsory education to all children of the age of six to fourteen years in a manner as the state may by law determine".

(b) **Substitution of New Article for Article 45.**—For Article 45 of the constitution, the following article shall be substituted, namely:

"45. Provision for early childhood care and education to children below the age of six years.— The state shall endeavour to provide early childhood care and education for all children until they complete the age of six years".

(c) **Amendment of Article 51 A.**—In Article 51A of the constitution, after clause(j), the following clause shall be added namely:

"(k) Who is a parent or guardian to provide opportunities for education to his child or ward, as the case may be, between the age of six and fourteen years".

The Right of children for free and compulsory education Bill having been passed by both Houses of parliament received the assent of the president on 26th August 2009. It came in the Statue Book as 'The Rights Of Children To Free And Compulsory Education Act 2009 (35 of 2009)'.

Significance of the Act

In several educational quarters the Education Act has been hailed as a great landmark legislation in the history of education in India. It is expected that its implementation will provide not only for free and compulsory education to every child between the age of 6 and 14 years of age but also help in raising standard of education. However, there are sceptics who do not find any weight in such arguments. It is true that the Act has raised high hopes but if past performance in free and compulsory education is any indicator it does not inspire much.

As a matter of fact every state has its own Education Act/ Code which includes almost all these provisions in the present Act. Nevertheless there is one major difference. Now it is backed by an Act of the Parliament. The Present Act specifies the duties of various stake holders in education i.e., the Central Government, the State Government, Local Authorities, the Parents and Teachers etc.

It appears a detailed mechanism will have to be worked out to demarc clearly the role of various authorities. From the contents of the Act, one is inclined to get the impression, that it will lead to more litigation and may become a haven for the legal community.

The Act comprising seven chapters specifies the rights of the child as also the duties of various agencies involved in the imparting of education to the child.

Main Provisions of the Act

- Provision of free and compulsory elementary education (class I to VIII) to every child.
- Ensuring availability of a neighbourhood school.
- Ensuring that the children belonging to weaker section are not discriminated against and prevented from pursuing and completing elementary education on any grounds;
- Providing infrastructure including school building, teaching staff and learning equipment;
- Providing special training facility.
- Ensuring and monitoring admission, attendance and completion of elementary education by every child;
- Ensuring good quality elementary education conforming to the standards and norms specified in the Schedule; (given separately).
- Ensuring timely prescribing of curriculum and courses of study for elementary education; and
- Providing training facility for teachers.
- Charging of no capitation fee.

- No screening procedure for admission.
- No denial for admission.
- No holding back in the same class.
- No expulsion.
- No physical punishment to the child.
- No mental harassment of the child.
- Appropriate condition of service teachers.
- Constitute of Managing Committee for every school committee.
- Suitable pupils teachers ratio.
- Filling of vacancy of teachers in time.
- Prohibition of deployment of teachers for non-education purposes.
- Prohibition of tuition by teachers.
- Monitoring child's right to education.
- Updating of curriculum from time to time and continuous and comprehensive evaluation.
- Constitution of National and State Advisory Councils.

Norms and Standards for a School

Sl. No.	*Item*	*Norms and Standards*	
1. Number of teachers:			
(a)	For Ist to 5th class	Admitted children	No. of teachers
		Up to 60	2
		61-90	3
		91-120	4
		121-200	5
		Above 150 children	5 plus 1 Head-teacher
		Above 200	Pupil-Teacher Ratio (excluding Head-teacher) shall not exceed forty.

(*Contd.*)

Sl. No.	*Item*	*Norms and Standards*
(b)	For sixth class to eighth class	(1) At least one teacher pre class so that there shall be at least one teacher each for— (i) Science and Mathematics; (ii) Social Studies; (iii) Languages. (2) At least one teacher for every thirty-five children. (3) Where admission of children is above one hundred-- (i) A full time head-teacher; (ii) Part time instructors for— (A) Art Education; (B) Health and Physical Education; (C) Work Education.
2. Building		All-weather building consisting of— (i) At ieast one class-room for every teacher and an office-cum-store-cum-Head teacher's room; (ii) Barrier-free access; (iii) Separate toilets for boys and girls; (iv) Safe and adequate drinking water facility to all children; (v) A kitchen where mid-day meal is cooked in the school; (vi) Playground.

General Observations:

1. Observations on Norms and standards of a school are taken of separately.
2. Science and mathematics should not be clubbed together.
3. No provision is made for co-scholastic or co-curricular activities.
4. Prescribed pupil-teacher ration is quite high.

In most of the public schools in Delhi overall pupil teacher ratio is 20 : 1. It is very clear that for maintaining standards in education pupil-teacher ratio must be less than 20. From the norms as given in Right to Education it is obvious that state schools which usually try to conform to norms will not be able to provide quality education.

EVALUATION OF THE ACT

Some Sections of the society have termed the Act as a landmark in the history of education while some consider it of no significance on the basis of past experience. According to Article 45, the target date for free and compulsory elementary education was fixed at 1960. Now there is no target date.

The present Art tends to create more problems than it solves. There are several issues which are to be resolved.

1. What are the financial implications of control and state governments for implementing the provisions?
2. Almost all state government and union Territories have their own Education Acts and Codes. With the control Art of 2009, there will have to be revised, since in the case of concurrency of Subjects, the control Act becomes supreme.
3. The Act does not provide for the exclusion of government school teachers from census, elections and disaster relief duties.
4. the document provides only for reimbursement of tuition fees of poor children enrolled in private schools but not other feels levied by most private schools. Unjustifiably, this burden may be passed on other students.
5. There is no provision in the legislation for decent salaries,/professional development, promotional avenues and social security for elementary teachers.
6. the Act is silent on the procedure of election of the chairperson and office bearers of the school management committees.
7. In the schedule of the Act detailing norms and standards for a school, teaching-learning equipment, library material, games and sports equipment, etc. are not satisfactory.
8. The right to education guarantees education of "equitable

quality" to children schools but this guarantee has no meaning unless the term "equitable quality" is defined.

9. The Act provides for no-detention policy. However, there should be some monitoring of children's academic and personal. However, For this purpose, it is better to hold back a pupil to repeat another year in the same class rather than pass him till class VIII.
10. The Act prohibits corporal punishment as well mental harassment of pupils. But mental harassment is left without a clear definition. This ambiguous part of the prohibitory provision could be misused against teachers by parents or school managements. The Act also prohibits expelling any child till class VIII. This should be viewed rationally. Deviant, repeatedly creating nuisance and vitiating the academic atmosphere and if counseling does not work, some action has to be taken.
11. A major factor relating to Right of children to free and compulsory Education, Act, 2009 is an economic one. For children to stay regularly in school requires huge efforts on the part of each family. Only families with certain welfare level can continue in the situations. Families affected by chronic employment and other disabilities encounter major difficulties. Estimates about below Poverty Line (BPL) VARY FROM ABOUT 26% TO ABOUT 60%. Children of these sections of the population provide economic and non-economic assistance to them. In thousands of cases, such children go to the school not for genuine education but for free mid-day meals. Thus the schools tend to become Dharmshalas. Their Attendance becomes very irregular. Moreover, it is not the obligation of the state to provide free and mid-day meals.

Another question arises. What will happen if the parents do not send their children to schools? Will the government punish them? Will the government set up a special litigation department?

All the factors perhaps demand a review of parameters of Right to Elementary Education.

APPENDIX I

THE RIGHT OF CHILDREN TO FREE AND COMPULSORY EDUCATION ACT, 2009

(35 of 2009)

[*26th August, 2009*]

An Act to provide for free and compulsory education to all children of the age of six to fourteen years.

BE it enacted by Parliament in the Sixtieth Year of the Republic of India as follows:—

CHAPTER I

PRELIMINARY

1. Short title, extent and commencement.—(1) This Act may be called the Right of Children to Free and Compulsory Education Act, 2009.

(2) It shall extend to the whole of India except the State of Jammu and Kashmir.

(3) It shall come into force on such date as the Central Government may, by notification in the Official Gazette, appoint.

2. Definitions.—In this Act, unless the context otherwise requires,—

(a) "appropriate Government" means—

(i) in relation to a school established, owned or controlled by the Central Government, or the administrator of the Union territory, having no legislature, the Central Government;

(ii) in relation to a school, other than the school referred to in sub-clause (i), established within the territory of—

(A) a State, the State Government;

(B) a Union territory having legislature, the Government of that Union territory;

(b) "capitation fee" means any kind of donation or contribution or payment other than the fee notified by the school;

(c) "child" means a male or female child of the age of six to fourteen years;

(d) "child belonging to disadvantaged group" means a child belonging to the Scheduled Caste, the Scheduled Tribe, the socially and educationally backward class or such other group having disadvantage owing to social, cultural, economical, geographical, linguistic, gender or such other factor, as may be specified by the appropriate Government, by notification;

(e) "child belonging to weaker section" means a child belonging to such parent or guardian whose annual income is lower than the minimum limit specified by the appropriate Government, by notification;

(f) "elementary education" means the education from first class to eighth class;

(g) "guardian", in relation to a child, means a person having the care and custody of that child and includes a natural guardian or guardian appointed or declared by a court or a statute;

(h) "local authority" means a Municipal Corporation or Municipal Council or Zila Parishad or Nagar Panchayat or Panchayat, by whatever name called, and includes such other authority or body having administrative control over the school or empowered by or under any law for the time being in force to function as a local authority in any city, town or village;

(i) "National Commission for Protection of Child Rights" means the National Commission for Protection of Child Rights constituted under Section 3 of the Commissions for Protection of Child Rights Act, 2005 (4 of 2006);

(j) "notification" means a notification published in the Official Gazette;

(k) "parent" means either the natural or step or adoptive father or mother of a child;

(l) "prescribed" means prescribed by rules made under this Act;

(m) "Schedule" means the Schedule annexed to this Act;

(n) "school" means any recognised school imparting

elementary education and includes—

(i) a school established, owned or controlled by the appropriate Government or a local authority;

(ii) an aided school receiving aid or grants to meet whole or part of its expenses from the appropriate Government or the local authority;

(iii) a school belonging to specified category; and

(iv) an unaided school not receiving any kind of aid or grants to meet its expenses from the appropriate Government or the local authority;

(o) "screening procedure" means the method of selection for admission of a child, in preference over another, other than a random method;

(p) "specified category", in relation to a school, means a school known as Kendriya Vidyalaya, Navodaya Vidyalaya, Sainik School or any other school having a distinct character which may be specified, by notification, by the appropriate Government;

(q) "State Commission for Protection of Child Rights" means the State Commission for Protection of Child Rights constituted under Section 3 of the Commissions for Protection of Child Rights Act, 2005 (4 of 2006).

CHAPTER II

RIGHT TO FREE AND COMPULSORY EDUCATION

3. Right of child to free and compulsory education.—(1) Every child of the age of six to fourteen years shall have a right to free and compulsory education in a neighbourhood school till completion of elementary education.

(2) For the purpose of sub-section (1), no child shall be liable to pay any kind of fee or charges or expenses which may prevent him or her from pursuing and completing the elementary education:

Provided that a child suffering from disability, as defined in Clause (i) of Section 2 of the Persons with Disabilities (Equal Opportunities, Protection and Full Participation) Act, 1996 (1 of 1996), shall have the right to pursue free and compulsory elementary education in accordance with the provisions of Chapter V of the said Act.

4. Special provisions for children not admitted to, or who have not completed, elementary education.—Where a child above six years of age has not been admitted in any school or though admitted, could not complete his or her elementary education, then, he or she shall be admitted in a class appropriate to his or her age:

Provided that where a child is directly admitted in a class appropriate to his or her age, then, he or she shall, in order to be at par with others, have a right to receive special training, in such manner, and within such time-limits, as may be prescribed:

Provided further that a child so admitted to elementary education shall be entitled to free education till completion of elementary education even after fourteen years.

5. Right of transfer to other school.—(1) Where in a school, there is no provision for completion of elementary education, a child shall have a right to seek transfer to any other school, excluding the school specified in sub-clauses (iii) and (iv) of Clause (n) of Section 2, for completing his or her elementary education.

(2) Where a child is required to move from one school to another, either within a State or outside, for any reason whatsoever, such child shall have a right to seek transfer to any other school, excluding the school specified in sub-clauses (iii) and (iv) of Clause (n) of Section 2, for completing his or her elementary education.

(3) For seeking admission in such other school, the Head-teacher or in-charge of the school where such child was last admitted, shall immediately issue the transfer certificate:

Provided that delay in producing transfer certificate shall not be a ground for either delaying or denying admission in such other school:

Provided further that the Head-teacher or in-charge of the school delaying issuance of transfer certificate shall be liable for disciplinary action under the service rules applicable to him or her.

CHAPTER III
DUTIES OF APPROPRIATE GOVERNMENT, LOCAL AUTHORITY AND PARENTS

6. Duty of appropriate Government and local authority to establish school.— For carrying out the provisions of this Act, the appropriate Government and the local authority shall establish, within such area or limits of neighbourhood, as may be prescribed, a school, where it is not so established, within a period of three years from the commencement of this Act.

7. Sharing of financial and other responsibilities.—(1) The Central Government and the State Governments shall have concurrent responsibility for providing funds for carrying out the provisions of this Act.

(2) The Central Government shall prepare the estimates of capital and recurring expenditure for the implementation of the provisions of the Act.

(3) The Central Government shall provide to the State Governments, as grants-in-aid of revenues, such percentage of expenditure referred to in sub-section (2) as it may determine, from time to time, in consultation with the State Governments.

(4) The Central Government may make a request to the President to make a reference to the Finance Commission under sub-clause (d) of Clause (3) of Article 280 to examine the need for additional resources to be provided to any State Government so that the said State Government may provide its share of funds for carrying out the provisions of the Act.

(5) Notwithstanding anything contained in sub-section (4), the State Government shall, taking into consideration the sums provided by the Central Government to a State Government under sub-section (3), and its other resources, be responsible to provide funds for implementation of the provisions of the Act.

(6) The Central Government shall—

(a) develop a framework of national curriculum with the help of academic authority specified under Section 29;

(b) develop and enforce standards for training of teachers;

(c) provide technical support and resources to the State Government for promoting innovations, researches, planning and capacity building.

8. Duties of appropriate Government.—The appropriate Government shall—

(a) provide free and compulsory elementary education to every child:

Provided that where a child is admitted by his or her parents or guardian, as the case may be, in a school other than a school established, owned, controlled or substantially financed by funds provided directly or indirectly by the appropriate Government or a local authority, such child or his or her parents or guardian, as the case may be, shall not be entitled to make a claim for reimbursement of expenditure incurred on elementary education of the child in such other school.

Explanation.—The term "compulsory education" means obligation of the appropriate Government to—

(i) provide free elementary education to every child of the age of six to fourteen years; and

(ii) ensure compulsory admission, attendance and completion of elementary education by every child of the age of six to fourteen years;

(b) ensure availability of a neighbourhood school as specified in Section 6;

(c) ensure that the child belonging to weaker section and the child belonging to disadvantaged group are not discriminated against and prevented from pursuing and completing elementary education on any grounds;

(d) provide infrastructure including school building, teaching staff and learning equipment;

(e) provide special training facility specified in Section 4;

(f) ensure and monitor admission, attendance and completion of elementary education by every child;

(g) ensure good quality elementary education

conforming to the standards and norms specified in the Schedule;

(h) ensure timely prescribing of curriculum and courses of study for elementary education; and

(i) provide training facility for teachers.

9. Duties of local authority.—Every local authority shall—

(a) provide free and compulsory elementary education to every child:

Provided that where a child is admitted by his or her parents or guardian, as the case may be, in a school other than a school established, owned, controlled or substantially financed by funds provided directly or indirectly by the appropriate Government or a local authority, such child or his or her parents or guardian, as the case may be, shall not be entitled to make a claim for reimbursement of expenditure incurred on elementary education of the child in such other school;

(b) ensure availability of a neighbourhood school as specified in Section 6;

(c) ensure that the child belonging to weaker section and the child belonging to disadvantaged group are not discriminated against and prevented from pursuing and completing elementary education on any grounds;

(d) maintain records of children up to the age of fourteen years residing within its jurisdiction, in such manner as may be prescribed;

(e) ensure and monitor admission, attendance and completion of elementary education by every child residing within its jurisdiction;

(f) provide infrastructure including school building, teaching staff and learning material;

(g) provide special training facility specified in Section 4;

(h) ensure good quality elementary education conforming to the standards and norms specified in the Schedule;

(i) ensure timely prescribing of curriculum and courses of study for elementary education;

(j) provide training facility for teachers;

(k) ensure admission of children of migrant families;
(l) monitor functioning of schools within its jurisdiction; and
(m) decide the academic calendar.

10. Duty of parents and guardian.—It shall be the duty of every parent or guardian to admit or cause to be admitted his or her child or ward, as the case may be, to an elementary education in the neighbourhood school.

11. Appropriate Government to provide for pre-school education.—With a view to prepare children above the age of three years for elementary education and to provide early childhood care and education for all children until they complete the age of six years, the appropriate Government may make necessary arrangement for providing free pre-school education for such children.

CHAPTER IV
RESPONSIBILITIES OF SCHOOLS AND TEACHERS

12. Extent of school's responsibility for free and compulsory education—(1) For the purposes of this Act, a school,—

(a) specified in sub-clause (i) of Clause (n) of Section 2 shall provide free and compulsory elementary education to all children admitted therein;
(b) specified in sub-clause (ii) of Clause (n) of Section 2 shall provide free and compulsory elementary education to such proportion of children admitted therein as its annual recurring aid or grants so received bears to its annual recurring expenses, subject to a minimum of twenty-five per cent;
(c) specified in sub-clauses (iii) and (iv) of Clause (n) of Section 2 shall admit in class I, to the extent of at least twenty-five per cent of the strength of that class, children belonging to weaker section and disadvantaged group in the neighbourhood and provide free and compulsory elementary education till its completion:

Provided further that where a school specified in Clause (n) of Section 2 imparts pre-school education, the provisions of Clauses (a) to (c) shall apply for admission to such pre-school education.

(2) The school specified in sub-clause (iv) of Clause (n) of Section 2 providing free and compulsory elementary education as specified in Clause (c) of sub-section (1) shall be reimbursed expenditure so incurred by it to the extent of per-child-expenditure incurred by the State, or the actual amount charged from the child, whichever is less, in such manner as may be prescribed:

Provided that such reimbursement shall not exceed per-child-expenditure incurred by a school specified in sub-clause (i) of Clause (n) of Section 2:

Provided further that where such school is already under obligation to provide free education to a specified number of children on account of it having received any land, building, equipment or other facilities, either free of cost or at a confessional rate, such school shall not be entitled for reimbursement to the extent of such obligation.

(3) Every school shall provide such information as may be required by the appropriate Government or the local authority, as the case may be.

13. No capitation fee and screening procedure for admission—(1) No school or person shall, while admitting a child, collect any capitation fee and subject the child or his or her parents or guardian to any screening procedure.

(2) Any school or person, if in contravention of the provisions of sub-section (1)—

(a) receives capitation fee, shall be punishable with fine which may extend to ten times the capitation fee charged;

(b) subjects a child to screening procedure, shall be punishable with fine which may extend to twenty-five thousand rupees for the first contravention and fifty thousand rupees for each subsequent contraventions.

14. Proof of age for admission—(1) For the purposes of admission to elementary education, the age of a child shall be determined on the basis of the birth certificate issued in accordance with the provisions of the Births, Deaths and Marriages Registration Act, 1886 (6 of 1886) or on the basis of such other document, as may be prescribed.

(2) No child shall be denied admission in a school for lack of age proof.

15. No denial of admission—A child shall be admitted in a school at the commencement of the academic year or within such extended period as may be prescribed:

Provided that no child shall be denied admission if such admission is sought subsequent to the extended period:

Provided further that any child admitted after the extended period shall complete his studies in such manner as may be prescribed by the appropriate Government.

16. Prohibition of holding back and expulsion—No child admitted in a school shall be held back in any class or expelled from school till the completion of elementary education.

17. Prohibition of physical punishment and mental harassment to child—(1) No child shall be subjected to physical punishment or mental harassment.

(2) Whoever contravenes the provisions of sub-section (1) shall be liable to disciplinary action under the service rules applicable to such person.

18. No school to be established without obtaining certificate of recognition—(1) No school, other than a school established, owned or controlled by the appropriate Government or the local authority, shall, after the commencement of this Act, be established or function, without obtaining a certificate of recognition from such authority, by making an application in such form and manner, as may be prescribed.

(2) The authority prescribed under sub-section (1) shall issue the certificate of recognition in such form, within such period, in such manner, and subject to such conditions, as may be prescribed:

Provided that no such recognition shall be granted to a school unless it fulfils norms and standards specified under Section 19.

(3) On the contravention of the conditions of recognition, the prescribed authority shall, by an order in writing, withdraw recognition:

Provided that such order shall contain a direction as to which of the neighbourhood school, the children studying in the derecognised school, shall be admitted:

Provided further that no recognition shall be so withdrawn without giving an opportunity of being heard to such school, in such manner, as may be prescribed.

(4) With effect from the date of withdrawal of the recognition under sub-section (3), no such school shall continue to function.

(5) Any person who establishes or runs a school without obtaining certificate of recognition, or continues to run a school after withdrawal of recognition, shall be liable to fine which may extend to one lakh rupees and in case of continuing contraventions, to a fine of ten thousand rupees for each day during which such contravention continues.

19. Norms and standards for school—(1) No school shall be established, or recognised, under Section 18, unless it fulfils the norms and standards specified in the Schedule.

(2) Where a school established before the commencement of this Act does not fulfil the norms and standards specified in the Schedule, it shall take steps to fulfil such norms and standards at its own expenses, within a period of three years from the date of such commencement.

(3) Where a school fails to fulfil the norms and standards within the period specified under sub-section (2), the authority prescribed under sub-section (1) of Section 18 shall withdraw recognition granted to such school in the manner specified under sub-section (3) thereof.

(4) With effect from the date of withdrawal of recognition under sub-section (3), no school shall continue to function.

(5) Any person who continues to run a school after the recognition is withdrawn, shall be liable to fine which may extend to one lakh rupees and in case of continuing contraventions, to a fine of ten thousand rupees for each day during which such contravention continues.

20. Power to amend Schedule—The Central Government may, by notification, amend the Schedule by adding to, or omitting therefrom, any norms and standards.

21. School Management Committee—(1) A school, other than a school specified in sub-clause (iv) of Clause (n) of Section 2, shall constitute a School Management Committee consisting of the elected representatives of the local authority, parents or guardians of children admitted in such school and teachers:

Provided that at least three-fourth of members of such Committee shall be parents or guardians:

Provided further that proportionate representation shall be given to the parents or guardians of children belonging to disadvantaged group and weaker section:

Provided also that fifty per cent of Members of such Committee shall be women.

(2) The School Management Committee shall perform the following functions, namely:—

(a) monitor the working of the school;

(b) prepare and recommend school development plan;

(c) monitor the utilisation of the grants received from the appropriate Government or local authority or any other source; and

(d) perform such other functions as may be prescribed.

22. School Development Plan—(1) Every School Management Committee, constituted under sub-section (1) of Section 21, shall prepare a School Development Plan, in such manner as may be prescribed.

(2) The School Development Plan so prepared under sub-section (1) shall be the basis for the plans and grants to be made by the appropriate Government or local authority, as the case may be.

23. Qualifications for appointment and terms and conditions of service of teachers—(1) Any person possessing such minimum qualifications, as laid down by an academic authority, authorised by the Central Government, by notification, shall be eligible for appointment as a teacher.

(2) Where a State does not have adequate institutions offering courses or training in teacher education, or teachers possessing minimum qualifications as laid down under sub-section (1) are not available in sufficient numbers, the Central Government may, if it deems necessary, by notification, relax the minimum qualifications required for appointment as a teacher, for such period, not exceeding five years, as may be specified in that notification:

Provided that a teacher who, at the commencement of this Act, does not possess minimum qualifications as laid down under sub-section (1), shall acquire such minimum qualifications within a period of five years.

(3) The salary and allowances payable to, and the terms and conditions of service of, teacher shall be such as may be prescribed.

24. Duties of teachers and redressal of grievances—(1) A teacher appointed under sub-section (1) of Section 23 shall perform the following duties, namely:—

(a) maintain regularity and punctuality in attending school;
(b) conduct and complete the curriculum in accordance with the provisions of sub-section (2) of Section 29;
(c) complete entire curriculum within the specified time;
(d) assess the learning ability of each child and accordingly supplement additional instructions, if any, as required;
(e) hold regular meetings with parents and guardians and apprise them about the regularity in attendance, ability to learn, progress made in learning and any other relevant information about the child; and
(f) perform such other duties as may be prescribed.

(2) A teacher committing default in performance of duties specified in sub-section (1), shall be liable to disciplinary action under the service rules applicable to him or her:

Provided that before taking such disciplinary action, reasonable opportunity of being heard shall be afforded to such teacher.

(3) The grievances, if any, of the teacher shall be redressed in such manner as may be prescribed.

25. Pupil-Teacher Ratio—(1) Within six months from the date of commencement of this Act, the appropriate Government and the local authority shall ensure that the Pupil-Teacher Ratio, as specified in the Schedule, is maintained in each school.

(2) For the purpose of maintaining the Pupil-Teacher Ratio under sub-section (1), no teacher posted in a school shall be made to serve in any other school or office or deployed for any non-educational purpose, other than those specified in Section 27.

26. Filling up vacancies of teachers—The appointing authority, in relation to a school established, owned, controlled or substantially financed by funds provided directly or indirectly by the appropriate Government or by a local authority, shall ensure that vacancy of teacher in a school under its control shall not exceed ten per cent, of the total sanctioned strength.

27. Prohibition of deployment of teachers for non-educational purposes—No teacher shall be deployed for any non-educational purposes other than the decennial population census, disaster relief duties or duties relating to elections to the local authority or the State Legislatures or Parliament, as the case may be.

28. Prohibition of private tuition by teacher—No teacher shall engage himself or herself in private tuition or private teaching activity.

CHAPTER V
CURRICULUM AND COMPLETION OF ELEMENTARY EDUCATION

29. Curriculum and evaluation procedure.—(1) The curriculum and the evaluation procedure for elementary education shall be laid down by an academic authority to be specified by the appropriate Government, by notification.

(2) The academic authority, while laying down the curriculum and the evaluation procedure under sub-section (1), shall take into consideration the following, namely:—

(a) conformity with the values enshrined in the Constitution;
(b) all round development of the child;
(c) building up child's knowledge, potentiality and talent;

(d) development of physical and mental abilities to the fullest extent;
(e) learning through activities, discovery and exploration in a child friendly and child-centered manner;
(f) medium of instructions shall, as far as practicable, be in child's mother tongue;
(g) making the child free of fear, trauma and anxiety and helping the child to express views freely;
(h) comprehensive and continuous evaluation of child's understanding of knowledge and his or her ability to apply the same.

30. Examination and completion certificate—(1) No child shall be required to pass any Board examination till completion of elementary education.

(2) Every child completing his elementary education shall be awarded a certificate, in such form and in such manner, as may be prescribed.

CHAPTER VI
PROTECTION OF RIGHT OF CHILDREN

31. Monitoring of child's right to education—(1) The National Commission for Protection of Child Rights constituted under Section 3, or, as the case may be, the State Commission for Protection of Child Rights constituted under Section 17, of the Commissions for Protection of Child Rights Act, 2005 (4 of 2006), shall, in addition to the functions assigned to them under that Act, also perform the following functions, namely:—

(a) examine and review the safeguards for rights provided by or under this Act and recommend measures for their effective implementation;
(b) inquire into complaints relating to child's right to free and compulsory education; and
(c) take necessary steps as provided under Sections 15 and 24 of the said Commissions for Protection of Child Rights Act.

(2) The said Commissions shall, while inquiring into any matters relating to child's right to free and compulsory education under Clause (c) of sub-section (1), have the same powers as assigned to them respectively under Section 14 and 24 of the said commissions for Protection of Child Rights Act.

(3) Where the State Commission for Protection of Child Rights has not been constituted in a State, the appropriate Government may, for the purpose of performing the functions specified in Clauses (a) to (c) of sub-section (1), constitute such authority, in such manner and subject to such terms and conditions, as may be prescribed.

32. Redressed of grievances—(1) Notwithstanding anything contained in Section 31, any person having any grievance relation to the right of a child under this Act may make a written complaint to the local authority giving jurisdiction.

(2) After receiving the complaint under sub-section (1), the local authority shall decide the matter within a period of three months after affording a reasonable opportunity of being heard to the parties concerned.

(3) Any person aggrieved by the decision of the local authority may prefer an appeal to the State Commission for Protection of Child Rights or the authority prescribed under sub-section (3) of Section 31, as the case may be.

(4) The appeal preferred under sub-section (3) shall be decided by State Commission for Protection of child Rights or the authority prescribed under sub-section (3) of Section 31, as the case may be, as provided under Clause (c) of sub-section (1) of Section 31.

33. Constitution of National Advisory Council—(1) The Central Government shall constitute, by notification, a national Advisory Council, consisting of such number of Members, not exceeding fifteen, as the Central Government may deem necessary, to be appointed from amongst persons having knowledge and practical experience in the field of elementary education and child development.

(2) The functions of the National Advisory Council shall be to advise the central Government on implementation of the provisions of the Act in an effective manner.

(3) The allowances and other terms and conditions of the appointment of members of the National Advisory Council shall be such as may be prescribed.

34. Constitution of State Advisory Council—(1) The state Government shall constitute, by notification, a State Advisory Council consisting of such number of Members, not exceeding fifteen, as the State Government may deem necessary, to be appointed from amongst persons having knowledge and practical experience in the field of elementary education and child development.

(2) The functions of the State Advisory Council shall be to advise the State Government on implementation of the provisions of the Act in an effective manner.

(3) The allowances and other terms and conditions of appointment of Members of the State Advisory Council shall be such as may be prescribed.

CHAPTER VII
MISCELLANEOUS

35. Power to issue directions.—(1) The Central Government may issue such guidelines to the appropriate Government or, as the case may be, the local authority, as it deems fit for the purposes of implementation of the provisions of this Act.

(2) The appropriate Government may issue guidelines and give such directions, as it deems fit, to the local authority or the School Management Committee regarding implementation of the provisions of this Act.

(3) The local authority may issue guidelines and give such directions, as it deems fit, to the School Management Committee regarding implementation of the provisions of this Act.

36. Previous sanction for prosecution—No prosecution for offences punishable under sub-section (2) of Section 13, sub-section (5) of Section 18 and sub-section (5) of Section 19 shall be instituted except with the previous sanction of an officer authorised in this behalf, by the appropriate Government, by notification.

37. Protection of action taken in good faith—No suit or

other legal proceeding shall lie against the Central Government, the State Government, the National Commission for Protection of Child Rights, the State Commission for Protection of Child Rights, the local authority, the School Management Committee or any person, in respect of anything which is in good faith done or intended to be done, in pursuance of this Act, or any rules or order made thereunder.

38. Power of appropriate Government to make rules—(1) The appropriate Government may, by notification, make rules, for carrying out the provisions of this Act.

(2) In particular, and without prejudice to the generality of the foregoing powers, such rules may provide for all or any of the following matters, namely:—

(a) the manner of giving special training and the time-limit thereof, under first proviso to Section 4;

(b) the area or limits for establishment of a neighbourhood school, under Section 6;

(c) the manner of maintenance of records of children up to the age of fourteen years, under Clause (d) of Section 9;

(d) the manner and extent of reimbursement of expenditure, under sub-section (2) of Section 12;

(e) any other document for determining the age of child under sub-section (1) of Section 14;

(f) the extended period for admission and the manner of completing study if admitted after the extended period, under Section 15;

(g) the authority, the form and manner of making application for certificate of recognition, under sub-section (1) of Section 18;

(h) the form, the period, the manner and the conditions for issuing Certificate of Recognition, under sub-section (2) of Section 18;

(i) the manner of giving opportunity of hearing under second proviso to sub-section (3) of Section 18;

(j) the other functions to be performed by School Management Committee; under Clause (d) of sub-section (2) of Section 21;

(k) the manner of preparing School Development Plan under sub-section (1) of Section 22;

(l) the salary and allowances payable to, and the terms and conditions of service of, teacher, under sub-section (3) of Section 23;

(m) the duties to be performed by the teacher under Clause (f) of sub-section (1) of Section 24;

(n) the manner of redressing grievances of teachers under sub-section (3) of Section 24;

(o) the form and manner of awarding certificate for completion of elementary education under sub-section (2) of Section 30;

(p) the authority, the manner of its constitution and the terms and conditions therefore, under sub-section (3) of Section 31;

(q) the allowances and other terms and conditions of appointment of Members of the National Advisory Council under sub-section (3) of Section 33;

(r) the allowances and other terms and conditions of appointment of Members of the State Advisory Council under sub-section (3) of Section 34.

(3) Every rule made under this Act and every notification issued under Sections 20 and 23 by the Central Government shall be laid, as soon as may be after it is made, before each House of Parliament, while it is in session, for a total period of thirty days which may be comprised in one session or in two or more successive sessions, and if, before the expiry of the session immediately following the session or the successive sessions aforesaid, both Houses agree in making any modification in the rule or notification or both Houses agree that the rule or notification should not be made, the rule or notification shall thereafter have effect only in such modified form or be of no effect, as the case may be; so, however, that any such modification or annulment shall be without prejudice to the validity of anything previously done under that rule or notification.

(4) Every rule or notification made by the State Government under this Act shall be laid, as soon as may be after it is made, before the State Legislatures.

THE SCHEDULE

(See Sections 19 and 25)

Norms and Standards for a School

NORMS AND STANDARDS FOR A SCHOOL

Sl. No.	*Item*			*Norms and Standards*
1.	Number of teachers:			
	(a)	For first class to fifth class	Admitted children	Number of teachers
			Up to Sixty	Two
			Between sixty-one to ninety	Three
			Between Ninety-one to one hundred and twenty	Four
			Between One hundred and twenty-one to two hundred	Five
			Above One hundred and fifty children	Five plus one Head-teacher
			Above Two hundred children	Pupil-Teacher Ratio (excluding Head-teacher) shall not exceed forty.
	(b)	For sixth class to eighth class	(1) At least one teacher per class so that there shall be at least one teacher each for— (i) Science and Mathematics; (ii) Social Studies; (iii) Languages.	
			(2) At least one teacher for every thirty-five children.	

(*Contd.*)

		(3) Where admission of children is above one hundred— (i) A full time head-teacher; (ii) Part time instructors for— (A) Art Education; (B) Health and Physical Education; (C) Work Education.
2.	Building	All-weather building consisting of— (i) At least one class-room for every teacher and an office-cum-store-cum-Head teacher's room; (ii) Barrier-free access; (iii) Separate toilets for boys and girls; (iv) Safe and adequate drinking water facility to all children; (v) A kitchen where mid-day meal is cooked in the school; (vi) Playground; (vii) Arrangements for securing the school building by boundary wall or fencing.
3.	Minimum number of working days/instructional hours in an academic year	(i) two hundred working days for first class to fifth class; (ii) two hundred and twenty working days for sixth class to eighth class; (iii) eight hundred instructional hours per academic year for first class to fifth class;

(*Contd.*)

		(iv) one thousand instructional hours per academic year for sixth class to eighth class
4.	Minimum number of working hours per week for the teacher	forty-five teaching including preparation hours.
5.	Teaching learning	shall be provided to each
6.	equipment Library	class as required. There shall be a library in each school providing newspaper, magazines and books on all subjects, including story-books.
7.	Play material, games and sports equipment	shall be provided to each class as required.

4

School Education: 'Report to the Nation'—National Knowledge Commission 2006-2009

INTRODUCTION

Reforms in school education are pivotal for creating an edifice on which a knowledge society can be structured. While India has witnessed significant progress in school education, the goal of universal access to elementary education has yet not been achieved. There are also wide disparities in access to school education between states, rural and urban areas, gender as well as different economic classes. In addition, issues of quality such as teacher training, curriculum, pedagogy, school infrastructure and learning outcomes need to be addressed on an immediate basis. There is also an urgent need to increase the resource allocation to school education.

CURRENT SCENARIO

Literacy

According to the 2001 Census, the literacy rate in India was 64.8 per cent and as per the NSS 61st Round Survey Report, the literacy rate was 67.3 per cent during 2004-05. Further, the gender gap in literacy is estimated to be roughly 20 per cent.

Schools

The number of primary schools in the country increased from 6.64 lakh in 2001-02 to 7.7 lakh in 2005-06. In the same period, the number of upper primary schools increased at a faster rate from 2.20 lakh to 2.9 lakh.

Table 4.1: Number of schools (in lakh) 2005-06

Primary	7.7
Upper primary	2.9
Secondary/Senior Secondary	1.6
Total	**12.2**

Source: Educational Statistics at a Glance, 2005-06, MHRD.

Enrolment

The total enrolment at the primary stage increased 7 times, from 19.2 million in 1950-51 to 130.8 million in 2004-05. In case of upper primary stage, it increased 17 times, from 3.1 million in 1950-51 to 51.2 million in 2004-05. The enrolment at the secondary/senior secondary increased by 25 times, from 1.5 million in 1950-51 to 37.1 million in 2004-05. However about 180 out of 581 districts in the DISE study (2004-05) reported a decline in primary enrolment.

Enrolment rates are particularly low in Bihar, Arunachal Pradesh, Jharkhand, Uttar Pradesh, Rajasthan and Madhya Pradesh, with overall enrolment rates below 80 per cent. There are wide rural-urban disparities, except in the Union Territories, North-eastern states, Kerala and to some extent Tamil Nadu. Gender disparities tend to be sharpest in states with low aggregate attendance rates (Fig. 4.1, 4.2 and 4.3).

The total Scheduled Castes enrolment at the primary (I-V), upper primary (VI-VIII) and secondary/senior secondary (IX-XII) stages of school education from 1980-81 to 2004-2005 increased by 2.25, 3.91 and 4.52 times respectively. The total Scheduled Tribes enrolment at the primary, upper primary and secondary/senior secondary stages of school education from 1980-81 to 2004-2005, increased by 2.94, 5.62 and 6.33 times respectively. Further, the average of 604 districts in 2005-06 indicates a gender parity index (GPI) of 0.92 in primary classes and 0.84 in case of enrolment in upper primary classes

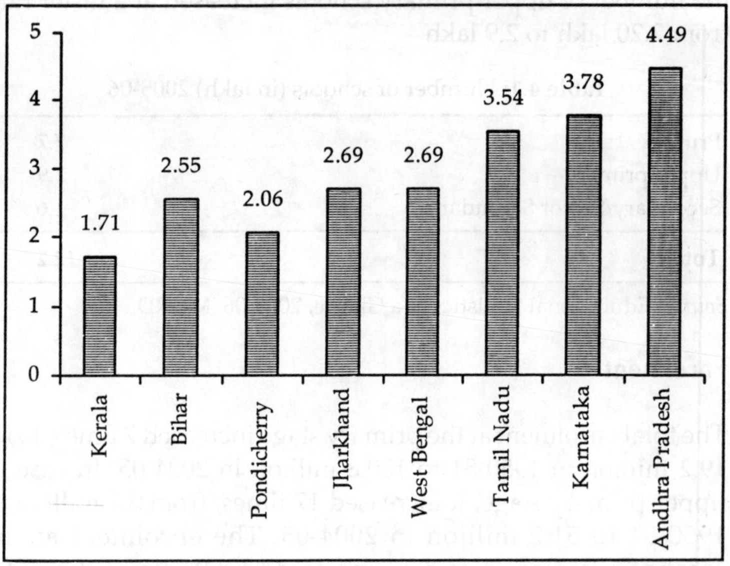

Fig. 4.1: Number of Schools per 1000 Students in the Relevant Age Group.

Source: Elementary Education in India, Analytical Report NUEPA, 2005-06.

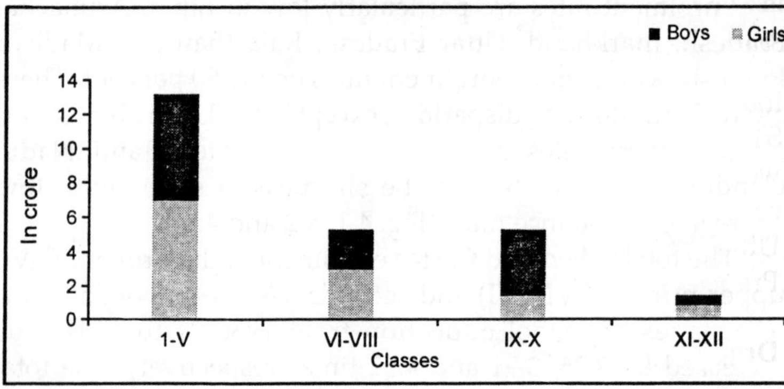

Fig. 4.2: Stage wise Enrolment (2005-06).

Source: National Level Statistics 2005-2006, MHRD.

compared to 0.91 and 0.83 in 2004-05. In 2003-04, GPI in primary and upper primary enrolment was 0.90 and 0.82 respectively. The social composition of out of elementary school children

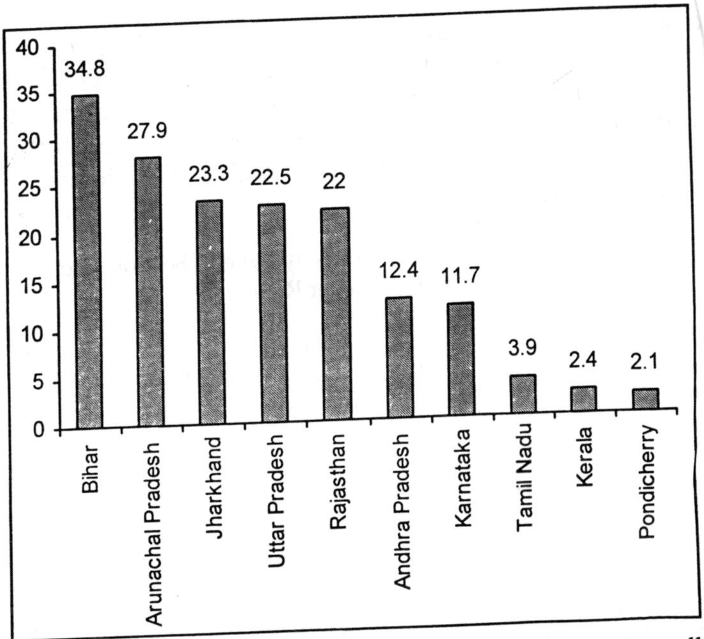

Fig. 4.3: Percentage of Students in the Relevant Age-group not enrolled in School.

Source: Elementary Education in India, Analytical Report, NUEPA, 2005-06.

indicates that 9.97 per cent of Muslim children, 9.54 per cent of STs, 8.17 per cent of SCs and 6.97 per cent of OBC children were out of school and an overwhelming majority (68.7 per cent) was concentrated in five States viz. Bihar (23.6 per cent), Uttar Pradesh (22.2 per cent), West Bengal (9 per cent), Madhya Pradesh (8 per cent) and Rajasthan (5.9 per cent).

Drop Outs

The drop-out rates represent percentage of pupils who drop out from a given grade or level of education in a given school year. The rate of drop outs has decreased from 64.9 per cent in 1960-61 to 29.00 per cent in 2004-2005 in primary classes. The rate of dropout which was 78.3 per cent in 1960-61, has come down to 50.84 per cent in 2004-2005 in the upper primary classes. Similarly, the dropout rate which was 82.5 per cent in 1980-81, has decreased to 61.92 per cent in 2004-2005 in the secondary classes, implying an improvement in retention rates. The drop-out rates at primary levels for SCs (34.2 per cent) and STs (42.3 per cent) are substantially higher than the national average (29 per cent).

Table 4.2: Number of Teachers by Type of Schools and Pupil: Teacher Ratio

Type of School	*No. of Teachers (in Lakh)*	*Percentage of Trained Teachers*	*Female Teachers Per 100 Male Teachers*	*Pupil Teacher Ratio*
Primary	21.8	86	65	46
Upper primary	16.7	87	67	34
High schools	11.2	89	61	32
Higher/Senior secondary	10.3	90	62	34

Source: National Level Statistics 2005-06, MHRD.

Teachers

The total number of teachers in primary schools increased from 5.38 lakh in 1950-51 to 21.6 lakh in 2004-2005 i.e. by more than four times. However, the number of teachers is still not adequate to meet the needs of the bourgeoning student population as is evident from the teacher pupil ratio.

During the year 1950-51 the pupil teacher ratio in primary schools was 1:24, in middle schools it was 1:20 and in higher/ higher secondary schools, the pupil teacher ratio was 1:21. By 2004-2005 this ratio had increased to 1:46 in primary schools; 1:35 in upper primary schools and 1:33 in secondary/senior secondary schools. Though the number of educational institutions has considerably increased after Independence and also the number of teachers, the higher pupil teacher ratio indicates that the increase in enrolment at each level is comparatively more than the increase in number of teachers.

The increased enrolment at various levels also underscores the need for opening of a greater number of educational institutions as well as employing more teachers for improving the quality of education.

Teacher Training Programmes

Teacher training has been identified as a crucial input for quality school education. However, the status of teacher training in India is a matter of great concern. According to DISE data, only 33 per cent of the teachers received in-service training in 2005-06. In 2002, 65467 men and 67096 women enrolled into teacher training courses in India. There are at present, about 571 DIETs, and DRCs, 104 Colleges of Advanced Teaching and 31 Institutes of Advanced Studies in Education, for pre-service and in-service training, functioning in the country.

Teacher Absenteeism

Teacher absenteeism has been identified as a major impediment to improvement in quality of school education. The PROBE survey in 242 villages across 5 north Indian states found that in about half the schools, there was no teaching activity at the time of the investigators' visit. It is significant that this pattern occurred even in cases where the school infrastructure (in terms of number of class rooms, teaching aids and even teacher-pupil ratio) was relatively good.

Infrastructure

There is a severe lack of basic infrastructure in schools in India. The PROBE (1999) survey, for instance, found the following with respect to government schools: (a) only a fourth of the sample schools had at least two teachers, two all-weather classrooms, and some teaching aids; (b) at the time of the investigator's visit, one-third of the headmasters were absent, one-third of the schools had a single teacher present, and about half of the schools had no teaching activity; (c) in many schools class students were systematically neglected. Similarly, the DISE survey found that only about 50 per cent of the schools had boundary walls, 33 per cent had electricity connections, and 52 per cent had playgrounds. These represent serious flaws in the schooling process.

Management

At present, government and local bodies own more than 90 per cent of the primary schools, 72 per cent of the upper primary schools and 39 per cent of the secondary schools. There are indications of a rise in the number of private unrecognised schools in India. According to the DISE Analytical Report as many as 63,411 and 1,26,110 schools in 2005-06 were being managed by the private aided and private unaided managements respectively. Together, they run a total of 1,89,521 schools (16.86 per cent). There is evidence to suggest that private schools are concentrated in areas where government funded schools are dysfunctional. Although the student profile of private schools is more economically advantaged, the rate of enrolment from poor families has also increased steadily. Findings from the MIMAP survey in India show that, of all school-enrolled children aged 5-10 years old living below the poverty line, 14.8 per cent attended private schools (8 per cent in rural and 36 per cent in urban India). The corresponding figures for ages 11-14 years and 15-17 years were 13.8 per cent and 7 per cent respectively (Pradhan and Subramaniam, 2000). Further, amongst the students from poor backgrounds in private schools, the majority are male.

Curriculum, Pedagogy and Learning Outcomes

An all India study *Annual Status of Education Report* (ASER) conducted by PRATHAM in 2006 found the levels in arithmetic and reading amongst primary school children to be surprisingly low. Close to 35 per cent of children in the 7-14 age group could not read a simple paragraph (grade 1 level difficulty) and almost 60 per cent of children could not read a simple story (grade 2 level). In Government Schools, 49.6 per cent of classes II-IV could not subtract (level 1), and 77.8 per cent could not complete sums in division. In private schools, 37.9 could not subtract (level 1) and 66.7 per cent could not finish division sums (level 2).

The situation in Tamil Nadu, Karnataka and Gujarat (where the schools function and where all provision related indicators are good) are far worse than in Bihar and Chhattisgarh (where indicators like teacher-pupil ratio, drop out rates are extremely high, and there are fewer schooling facilities). The high failure rates, especially among the rural, economically weaker and socially deprived children, forces one to critically review the whole system of evaluation and examination.

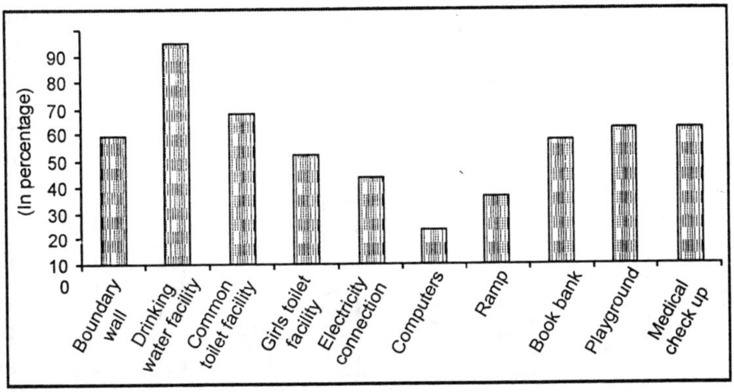

Fig. 4.4: Percentage of Schools with Basic Facilities.

Source: Elementary Education in India, Analytical Report 2006-07.

It is widely recognised that there is a need to shift focus from rote learning from textbooks to developing basic skills and the ability of students to apply their learning to real situations. Also creativity, problem-solving ability and encouragement for construction of knowledge based on students' own experiences needs to be promoted. Introducing accountability and developing other measures to improve teaching quality at the primary level needs to be thought of. The National Policy on Education (NPE), 1986 postulated that the examination system should be recast so as to ensure a method of assessment that is a valid and reliable measure of student development and a powerful instrument for improving teaching and learning be developed.

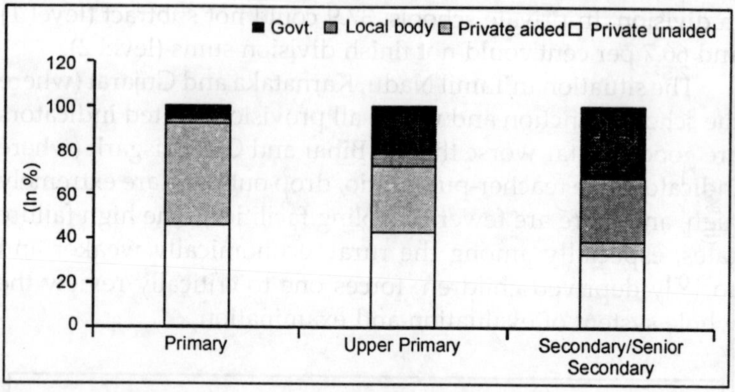

Fig. 4.5: Management-wise Percentage of Schools.

Source: National Level Statistics 2005-06, MHRD.

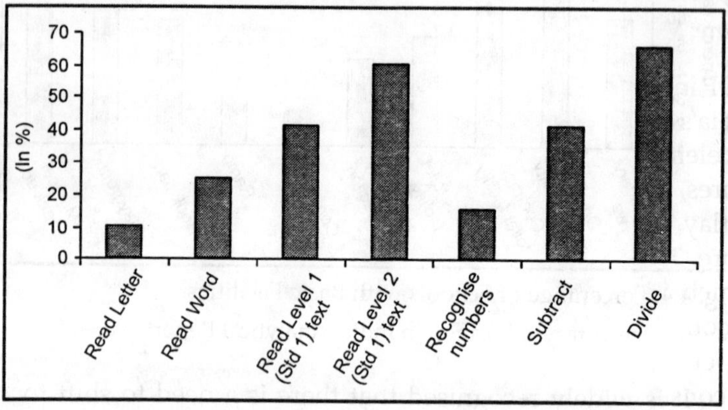

Fig. 4.6: Percentage of Children (Class I to VIII) who cannot.

Source: *Annual Status of Education Report* (Rural) 2006.

Government Funding

The share of public expenditure on education has been declining steadily and was 3.5 per cent in 2004-05. The share of elementary education was Rs. 40,000 crores out of almost 100,000 crores allotted to education. This amount is insufficient to provide universal elementary education of eight years for every child in the age group 6-14 years. It is also less than the proportion of

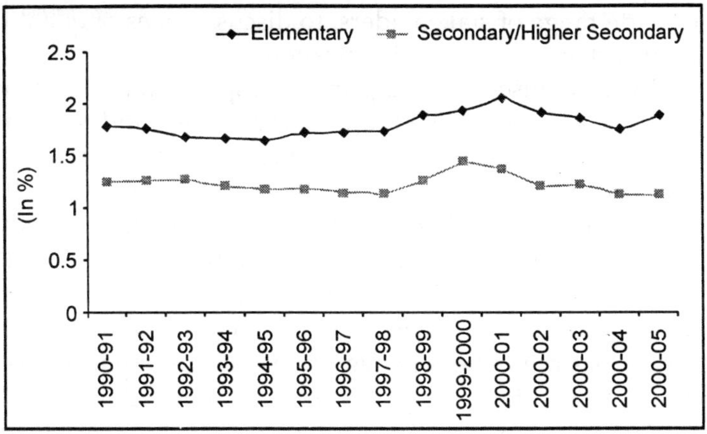

Fig. 4.7: Expenditure on Education as a Percentage of GDP.
Source: MHRD.

GDP invested in education in many other developing countries. India's total expenditure on school education for the year 2005-06, elementary and secondary combined was around Rs. 78,661 crores, amounting to only 2.46 per cent of GDP. The Tenth Plan outlay for Elementary Education and Literacy was Rs. 30,000 crore. The actual expenditure has been Rs. 48,201 crore, out of which SSA (Rs. 28,077 crore) and MDM (Rs. 13,827 crore) account for 88 per cent. The graph below shows public expenditure on education from year 1992-93 to 2005-06 in 1993-94 constant prices. The percentage allocation for education was around 3.5 per cent of GDP until the late 1990s, rose to more than 4 per cent at the turn of the decade but has since declined to 3.75 per cent of GDP.

MAJOR OBSERVATIONS AND RECOMMENDATIONS ON SCHOOL EDUCATION

Ensuring quality school education to all is the foundation upon which any further advances towards a knowledge society must be based. Noting the crucial importance of school education, the National Knowledge Commission held a series of workshops and consultations around the country involving a very wide range of stakeholders, to discuss issues of quantity, quality and access in school education.

NKC recognises that the primary responsibility for school education is borne by the State Governments, and therefore any policy changes must be with the full participation and involvement of the states. Nevertheless, NKC believes that positive changes in systems of schooling will require the active involvement of the Central Government as well as State Governments, not only in the matter of providing resources but also in promoting organisational and other changes.

NKC has a number of suggestions and recommendations covering the different aspects of school education, but the essential thrust can be summarised in terms of more resources, more decentralisation and more flexibility.

1. Central Legislation for the Right to Education, Backed by Financial Commitment

NKC endorses the speedy enactment of a central legislation that will ensure the right of all children in the country to good quality school education up to Class VIII, supported with financial commitments of the Central and State Governments. This obviously requires substantially increased public spending for both elementary and secondary school education, which must be seen as a priority area for spending. Currently school education is highly segmented, even in government-run institutions, as a result of the parallel track of "education centres" in some states. These separate systems must be integrated to give all children access to schools of acceptable quality, which will obviously require additional spending.

2. More Flexibility in Disbursal of Funds

However, there is a strong case for changes in the manner in which such expenditure is incurred. The current norms for central government disbursal to states of funds for [including for Sarva Shiksha Abhiyan (SSA)] the planned SUCCESS programme for secondary education and other central schemes, are too rigid and must be made more flexible. NKC strongly recommends a system of funds transfer and accounting that will allow for regional and other differences as well as changing requirements over time, and thereby allow State Governments to use the resources in the most effective way. There should also be greater flexibility in disbursing funds down to the school level and a greater degree of autonomy of local level management in the use of funds. The norms and rules should allow schools to adapt to local conditions and meet particular requirements of their students.

3. Decentralisation and Greater Local Autonomy

Community participation is an important instrument to ensure accountability and improve the day-to-day functioning of schools. This in turn means that the management of schools, including the use and management of funds, should be decentralised to local authorities as far as possible, whether they be panchayats, Village Education Committees or municipalities, and to School Boards that have representation of all stakeholders including parents.

4. Expansion of Functional Literacy

NKC would like to stress the continuing importance of a focus on expanding functional literacy among the population. Illiteracy remains a major problem, even among the age group 15-35 years, and therefore literacy programmes must be expanded rather than reduced, and given a different focus that is directed towards improving life skills and meeting felt needs, especially (but not only) among the youth.

5. Planning for School Infrastructure

It is important to remember that land is an essential requirement of schools, and this requirement is likely to increase in the near future given the expansion implied by demographic changes and need to ensure universal schooling. Therefore, urban master plans and local development plans must explicitly incorporate the physical requirements for schooling, including provisions for playgrounds and other school facilities.

6. Enabling and Regulating Mechanisms for Private Schools

Since private schools play an important role in the provision of education, there is need for both enabling and regulating mechanisms to be developed and strengthened for them. There should be transparent, norm-based and straightforward procedures for the recognition of private schools, to reduce harassment and bureaucratic delay. There should also be transparent criteria as for the disbursement of aid from the government to some self-financing schools, especially those which cater to underprivileged children, and clear norms with respect to the ability of school managements to raise resources from other sources. The monitoring of private schools, in terms of ensuring a transparent admissions process, regulation of fee structures, as well as meeting minimum set standards for quality of teaching and infrastructure, also requires attention. The possibility of greater exchange between schools, including mentoring of one school by another, should be allowed and encouraged.

7. Database on School Education

Educational planning and monitoring are made much more difficult because of the lack of comprehensive and accurate data on schools, school-age children and actual attendance of both students and teachers. The collection and speedy dissemination of accurate and current data on schooling must be made a priority. It is necessary to create a complete database on schools and school-age children so as to track the actual coverage and quality of schooling at different levels, and to make it widely available in a timely manner. Such data collection may be made an essential part of the fund allocation for school education, with appropriate institutional mechanisms.

8. More Co-ordination between Departments

The multiplicity of management structures and government departments that currently governs schooling creates confusion, unnecessary replication and possibly inconsistent strategies across different schools. There must be greater co-ordination between different departments of government on school education policy, even while ensuring more autonomy to the local management of schools.

9. National Evaluation Body for Monitoring Quality

Educational administration also needs to be more conscious of actual learning outcomes at different levels, which will determine both policy and functioning. NKC therefore proposes a national evaluation body to monitor the quality of both government and private schools, using a results-based monitoring framework based on a short list of monitorable criteria that include both process and outcome indicators.

10. Revamping School Inspection

The system of school inspection needs to be revamped and revitalised, with a greater role for local stakeholders and greater transparency in the system. The solution does not lie in simply expanding the system—rather, we need to develop systems to ensure meaningful monitoring, including provision of greater facilities to school inspectors, a separation of inspection of qualitative and administrative aspects, transparency in the criteria of inspection, and greater involvement of local stakeholders.

11. Teachers and Teacher Training

Teachers are the single most important element of the school system, and the country is already facing a severe shortage of qualified and motivated school teachers at different levels. It is urgent to restore the dignity of school teaching as a profession and provide more incentives for qualified and committed teachers. Non-teaching official duties such as electoral activities should not be allowed to interfere with the teaching process. Forums that allow and encourage teachers to exchange ideas, information and experiences, including a web-based portal, should be developed.

At the same time, there should be transparent systems for ensuring accountability of school teachers. As far as possible, teachers should be recruited to particular schools.

The training of teachers is a major area of concern at present, since both pre-service and in-service training of school teachers is extremely inadequate and also poorly managed in most states. Pre-service training needs to be improved and differently regulated in both public and private institutions, while systems for in-service training require expansion and major reform that allows for greater flexibility.

12. Reforms in the Curriculum and Examination System

Curriculum reform remains a critically important issue in almost all schools. School education must be made more relevant to the lives of children. There is need to move away from rote-learning to understanding concepts, developing good comprehension and communication skills and learning how to access knowledge independently. This also requires substantial changes in the examination system, especially at Board level but also earlier.

13. Use of Information and Communication Technology

Wherever feasible, ICT should be made more accessible to teachers, students and administration for learning, training, research, administration, management, monitoring etc. This requires the provision of more facilities such as computers as well as connectivity and broadband facilities. Computer-aided learning also requires training of teachers and other staff in order to make the best use of technology.

14. English Language Teaching

Proficiency in English is widely perceived as an important avenue for employment and upward mobility, which also greatly facilitates the pursuit of higher education. The incorporation of English into the curriculum through the teaching of English as a language in Class I and teaching of one other subject in English medium in later classes requires making pedagogical changes to contextualise language learning, increasing the availability of English language teachers and providing more bilingual and supplementary teaching materials. At the same time, multi-linguality must be promoted and language issues must be explicitly taken on board in designing school curricula and methods of pedagogy.

15. Interventions to Ensure Access of Educationally Deprived Categories

Special interventions are necessary to ensure greater access to education of educationally deprived categories, and some proposals for this are developed in more detail in the accompanying Note. Obviously, specific measures are required to ensure greater enrolment and retention of girl students. Education of SC children must be a priority, which necessitates both flexibility of approach and avoidance of discrimination. The access of children from Scheduled Tribes requires more flexible and sensitive schooling strategies. Language issues must be explicitly taken on board in designing school curricula and methods of pedagogy. Special strategies are required to ensure greater access to schools for children in backward regions, remote locations and difficult terrains. Official strategies for ensuring better access of Muslim children to schooling are excessively focused on madrasas which cater to only a tiny minority of such children; the emphasis should be on creating enabling conditions for Muslim children in the general school system. Children of seasonal migrants require special conditions and efforts to ensure continuous access to schooling. Similarly, labouring children require incentives and bridge courses. The needs of physically disadvantaged children, as well as teachers, have to be factored in more thoroughly in provisions for school education.

There is wide diversity across states in terms of progress towards achieving universal elementary education, and also diversity within states with respect to the quality of school education. But NKC believes that these proposals, which require the active involvement of the Central Government as well as State Governments, will go some way in terms of ensuring universal access to elementary education, wider access to secondary education as well as better quality and greater relevance of all schooling. Given the strong synergies between this and other areas such as libraries, translation, knowledge networks etc, these suggestions should be seen in conjunction with other recommendations that have already been made in these other areas, as part of a systematic set of knowledge initiatives for the young.

NOTE ON SCHOOL EDUCATION

The Prime Minister has repeatedly emphasised that ensuring quality school education to all is one of the most important priorities of the government, and the National Knowledge Commission has also recognised the crucial significance of this as the foundation upon which any further advances must be based. NKC has held a series of workshops around the country, addressing issues of quantity, quality and access in school education, and tried to involve a very wide range of stakeholders in the consultations.

NKC recognises that the primary responsibility for school education is borne by the State Governments, and therefore any policy changes must be with the full participation and involvement of the states. Also, there is wide diversity across states in terms of progress towards achieving universal elementary education, and also diversity within states with respect to the quality of school education. Nevertheless, NKC believes that positive changes in systems of schooling that will ensure universal access to elementary education, wider access to secondary education as well as better quality and greater relevance of all schooling, will require the active involvement of the Central Government as well as State Governments. Such involvement is necessary not only in the matter of providing resources but also in promoting organisational and other changes. NKC has a number of suggestions and recommendations covering the different aspects of school education, but the essential thrust can be summarised in terms of **more resources, more decentralisation and more flexibility.** Outlined below are the most important areas of possible intervention. NKC is aware that while some proposals are new, other recommendations have found expression in different ways in previous reports and studies. However, NKC has chosen to reiterate them because they are still crucial and relevant.

NKC would also like to emphasise that there are very strong synergies between these recommendations for school education and other proposals of NKC with respect to libraries, translation, networks, language in schools and vocational education. These suggestions should therefore be seen in conjunction with the other recommendations that have already been made in these areas, as part of a systematic set of knowledge initiatives for the young.

Quantity and Resources

Substantially Increased Public Spending is Required for Both Elementary and Secondary Education

NKC strongly endorses the speedy enactment of a central legislation that will ensure the right of all children in the country to good quality school education up to Class VIII. We also believe that this should be extended to cover universal schooling up to Class X as soon as possible. NKC has emphasised that a vibrant, good quality and universally accessible government school system is the basic foundation upon which the schooling system in the country must rest.

Therefore this must be supported with a financial commitment of the Central Government, in such a way as to ensure that the right to quality school education is provided to all children of the country, regardless of which state they are residing in. This necessarily requires a significant expansion of the resources to be provided to elementary school education. While the government has increased allocations for school expenditure, the amounts are still far below what is required to achieve universal school education of reasonable quality for all. This is even more true because of the need to upgrade the "Education Centres" that are operating in many states to proper schools that meet all the norms in terms of trained teachers, minimum facilities etc. Therefore NKC strongly recommends a substantial increase in Central Government allocation.

NKC has already expressed concern on the recent decision of the central government to reduce the central funding for the Sarva Shiksha Abhiyan (SSA) from 75 per cent to 50 per cent. This may lead to a sharp curtailment of progress towards universal school education, especially in the more backward states where the gap is greater. It is worth noting that State Governments are already incurring the bulk of school education expenditure. NKC strongly feels that, in addition to 50 per cent of SSA funds, the Centre should provide all the additional funding required to ensure the Right to Education in those states where the state government is already spending at least 15 per cent of its total budget on school education.

At the same time, the importance of increased spending on secondary education is greater than ever before. There is a huge shortage of middle and secondary schools, which is one of the important reasons for the low rates of retention after Class V. Currently, secondary education is massively under-funded, which in turn creates not only absolute shortages but also problems of inadequate quality in many government secondary and higher secondary schools. The aim should be to reach universal secondary school education within a maximum of 10 years. Given the demographics, this implies that expenditure on secondary schooling must be increased by several multiples within the next two years, indeed by at least five times the current level if the CABE estimates are used. Currently, many primary schools are being upgraded to secondary school status, without provision of sufficient teachers, rooms and other pedagogical requirements, which severely comprises on the quality of such secondary education. The norms for secondary schools, which include not only provision for specialised subject teachers but also for science labs, counselling etc., must be strictly adhered to when new schools are created and when primary schools are upgraded.

Urban Planning and Local Planning must Explicitly Incorporate the Physical Requirements for Schooling, Including Provisions for Playgrounds and Other School Facilities

It is important to remember that land is an essential requirement of schools, and this requirement is likely to increase in the near future given the expansion required by demographic changes and the need to ensure universal schooling. In the context of rapid urbanisation, it has been found that urban conglomerations often come up without adequate provision for ensuring the physical space required for schools in the vicinity. This is particularly a problem in new settlements with quickly increasing density of population, not only in large cities but also in smaller towns and fast growing villages. This makes it difficult to establish schools where required, and to ensure that schools are able to provide all the necessary facilities including sports fields etc. It is essential that the urban land use policies and regulations in all states and municipalities explicitly factor in the physical requirements of schools in areas of a certain population density.

Similarly in rural areas, there must be adequate provision for land for setting up schools in areas that surpass a certain population density. In rural areas with low population density, difficult terrain or extreme climatic conditions, the government may consider setting up residential schools, which could also address the problem of migrant labourers and nomadic populations.

The Norms for Central Government Disbursal to States of Sarva Shiksha Abhiyan (SSA) Funds and Other Central Schemes for School Education are too Rigid and must be made More Flexible

The current system of funds transfer and the accounting rules create unnecessary rigidities that often do not allow the State Governments to use the money in the most efficient or desirable way, and also lead to less than complete utilisation of the budgetary allocation.

Some of these problems include:

- very rigid norms on unit costs and what is allowed in terms of spending, that do not recognise the diverse requirements of different states or particular regions;
- inadequate financial provisions for infrastructure such as buildings etc, especially for some states and cities, which leads to the creation of poor quality infrastructure;
- an inflexible accounting system that does not allow transferring funds across heads to meet particular or changing requirements, and therefore inhibits full utilisation and also prevents synergies from developing;
- insufficient allocation for repair and maintenance of infrastructure;
- treating rural and urban schools in the same manner even though the requirements are often very different (for example, urban government schools may require different infrastructure and facilities in order to attract students); and
- treating all districts and geographical areas in the same manner regardless of the degree of backwardness, topographical conditions etc. (This is especially a problem for schools in hilly or heavily forested areas or those with poor physical connectivity for which per capita allocations are the same as for other more accessible areas);
- problems in the timing of fund transfer, as well as uncertainties in fund provision created by the insistence

on matching funds and the fact that plan ceilings keep changing every year.

NKC strongly recommends a less rigid and more flexible system of funds transfer and accounting that will allow for regional and other differences as well as changing requirements over time, and thereby allow State Governments to use the resources in the most effective way. This recommendation is both for the SSA and for the planned SUCCESS programme for secondary education, and also for other centrally sponsored schemes relating to school education.

There should be Greater Flexibility in Disbursing Funds Down to the School Level and a Greater Degree of Autonomy of Local Level Management in the Use of Funds

Even within the states, the norms for fund disbursal and the requirements are often very time consuming and breed delays and unnecessary rigidities. There should be recognition of differences in per capita resource requirement according to particular criteria, such as geographical and spatial characteristics, the presence of children with special needs, seasonality and other features.

In addition, there is a strong case for providing greater autonomy to local level management of schools, including locally elected bodies, school boards, Village Education Committees etc., in the use and management of funds, subject to some overall criteria. Within the stipulated norms for expenditure, there should be scope for greater flexibility in the use of funds in response to local needs and local innovation.

There Should be Transparent, Norm-based and Straightforward Procedures for the Recognition of Private Schools, As Well As for the Disbursement of Aid from the Government to Self Financing Schools and the Ability of School Management to Raise Resources from Other Sources

Private schools play a significant role in dispensing school education. It is estimated by NUEPA that around 15 per cent of schools in the country are privately owned and managed, while in some urban areas, private schools cater to a very large proportion of school going children. Their role must be recognised, and those providing quality education should be encouraged, especially when they cater to less privileged children.

However, many private schools have identified the time consuming procedures for renewal of recognition from the government, which have to be undertaken at relatively frequent intervals, as a source of harassment. It is necessary to simplify the rules and reduce the multiplicity of clearances required for private schools, by developing a modality for coordinated point of clearance as far as possible. There is also a case for increasing the time period for which recognition is granted to such schools, especially those with a proven track record. Transparency in dealings between the government and private schools will also be aided if the information on rules and criteria for registration and the results of all school applications for granting of recognition are made public in an accessible form, including by making the relevant information available on websites.

Those charitable schools that provide quality education to children from underprivileged and marginalised sections of society deserve encouragement, and may be considered for receipt of government resources, according to transparent and norm-based procedures. However, all mechanisms of government aid disbursement to privately run schools should be transparently conducted and according to defined norms.

There is a widespread perception that government rules currently reduce the ability of school managements to raise resources from other sources for the expansion of infrastructure or to provide other facilities. This varies across states, but in general in most states the current system does allow schools to raise funds from donations, resources extended from the panchayat and other sources. However, it is important to ensure that the available flexibility for school management to raise resources should be widely known and publicised. In addition, innovative methods of raising additional resources could be allowed and encouraged. For example, schools, particularly in urban areas, could use assets such as buildings during non-school hours to generate additional funds to improve the quality of facilities.

Illiteracy Remains a Major Problem, and Therefore Literacy Programmes cannot be Ignored or Given Less Importance. Expenditure on the National Literacy Mission (NLM) must be Expanded Rather than Reduced, and Given a Different Focus

The shift in policy focus from the National Literacy Mission (NLM) to the Sarva Shiksha Abhiyan has led to a declining emphasis on the need to ensure universal functional literacy. However, according to the 2001 Census, a significant proportion of the population—nearly half of all females and one-quarter of males—remains functionally illiterate. According to the NSSO, a significant proportion of households in 2004-05 (more than a quarter in rural India and nearly 10 per cent in urban India) have no literate member. The lack of functional literacy is much more marked among women, those residing in backward areas and those from marginalised social groups. Also, a significant proportion of young people—around 30 per cent of the age-cohort of 15-35 years—is functionally illiterate, since they were too old to benefit from the SSA and also slipped through the net of the literacy programmes. This is of great concern because such people will continue to be active citizens for the next half century and therefore, must not be denied the capacities and opportunities that come from being literate.

NKC therefore recommends the following measures for literacy:

- Ensure greater funds for the NLM, including provision for more pedagogical resources including not only ICT but also locally generated teaching material as well as local hiring of temporary staff wherever required.
- Encourage the NLM to shift to creating Continuing Education Centres in both rural and urban areas, to impart functional literacy that is of relevance and interest to those who are currently illiterate or recently

literate, as well as provide further learning material and other resources and facilities to the newly literate.

- Orient the post-literacy and continuing education programmes to the emotional, physical and psychological needs of adults rather than children, incorporating issues regarding citizens' rights, human rights, sex education, health and livelihood government programmes etc.
- Use a variety of methods to ensure functional literacy, which combine more centralised schemes based on ICT and other new technology with continuous work at the local level based on a clear institutional structure. While new technologies such as ICT provide important new methods for imparting literacy in a short time, they necessarily have a limited role. They cannot be seen as standalone quick-fix solutions, but must be combined with other methods.
- Move to a sustainable system of literacy generation that does not rely on underpaid "volunteer" labour alone, which therefore involves budgetary provision for better remuneration for literacy workers.
- Create synergies between NLM and the proposed Skill Development Mission, while taking local needs and field requirements into account. For example, in some primarily agrarian economies, undue emphasis on industrial skills in ITIs may be incongruous while horticultural and animal husbandry skills may be more relevant.

Early Childhood Education is Extremely Important and must be Universalised

There are two aspects to ensuring the universalisation of early schooling and pre-school education. The first is the systematic extension of balwadis with trained staff to handle child pedagogy. The second is the provision for one year of pre-schooling in all institutions of elementary education. Both of these have implications for resource allocation and recruitment of the requisite staff.

The Collection and Speedy Dissemination of Accurate and Current Data on Schooling Must be Made a Priority It is Necessary to Create a Complete Database on Schools and School-age Children So as to Track the Actual Coverage and Quality of Schooling at Different Levels, and to Make it Widely Available in a Timely Manner. Such Data Collection may be Made an Essential Part of the Fund Allocation for School Education, with Appropriate Institutional Mechanisms

India has an extensive and regular mechanism of data collection for primary education. However, its methodology and use leave much to be desired. For example, at present there is no reliable method for establishing which children are in schools. Data collection is too extensive, time-intensive and done almost entirely by teachers, rather than by independent and specialised personnel. There is minimal cross tabulation, coordination and cross referencing of data. The results are typically revealed to administrators, schools etc. too late to be relevant—often several years after the survey takes place. It is immensely difficult even for stakeholders, as well as other concerned citizens, to access the data lying with official sources, despite repeated requests.

It is necessary to have a system to provide reliable school education statistics which must be transparently formulated and freely available to all. This requires mechanisms that are incorporated into the funding for all school education, at central and state government levels. These would ensure data collection and access, provide up to date information as rapidly as possible, make it more relevant for planning and implementation and more accessible for everyone. The following goals are relevant in this context:

- The process of data collection must be streamlined, made less time consuming and more relevant.
- A comprehensive mapping is required of schools and children of school-going age, so as to have accurate information on which children in which localities are enrolled, and attending which schools, as well as those not enrolled. This would also map out localities where there are high rates of drop out and/or non-enrolment.

- A tracking mechanism for all school children should be set up, to track their individual school going status, and progress in school. This tracking should cover both government schools and private schools. This would ensure universal access for children in all locations, as well as for girls and specific categories. A tracking mechanism will also facilitate checking for drop outs and related problems, and allow for speedy intervention to address such problems. It should be noted that there are already ongoing initiatives in this regard in some states, which can be replicated and scaled up.
- Data collected for the purposes of planning must provide all the relevant information. This is also important with respect to information on infrastructure provision: for example, the number of rooms should also mention whether these are electrified; where availability of toilets is described, there should also be information on the availability of water in the toilets.
- Safeguards must be instituted against "creative readjustment" of data, which is a common problem given the structure of incentives and the fact that the data are most often provided by the teachers or school management. This requires that data should be collected by independent agencies as far as possible, or necessarily subject to frequent and random cross-checks.
- ICT must be integrated for data collation and management, wherever required. A local area network with digital entry provisions could be set up to make it easier for the teachers and others who provide and use the data.
- The data thus collected must be freely available and easily accessible, provided on dedicated websites in addition to the usual means of publication.
- More specialised micro level surveys and research should be commissioned. There should also be attempts to bring together other relevant research for easy access by practitioners.

Quality and Management

Currently School Education is Highly Segmented, Even in Government Run Institutions, as a Result of the Parallel Track of "Education Centres" in Some States. These Separate Systems must be Integrated to Give all Children Access to Schools of Acceptable Quality. This will Require Additional Spending

In a number of states, funds under various schemes (SSA, EGS and AIE) were used to create "Education Centres" (Shiksha Kendras) rather than proper schools. These typically involve "teachers" who are essentially local women who have just passed Class VIII (or even Class V in some cases) and are paid between Rs. 1000 to Rs. 3000 per month in the different states. They typically receive no training or a two-week training at best, and may have to teach multi-grade classes often in single rooms. The proportion of children in such schools varies widely, but the all India average amounts to around 16 per cent of total enrolment in primary education, according to the Planning Commission. All such children are described in the official statistics as enrolled in schools, even though going to an Education Centre cannot be treated as school enrolment on par with the proper schools, and such instructors do not meet the required norms for teachers. Currently, State Governments allow these parallel (and deeply unequal) systems of schooling to continue to be run by different departments—"proper schools" by the Education Department, and education centres under the panchayats and therefore by the Panchayat Department.

The need to integrate these two parallel systems must be explicitly recognised. This requires special budgetary allocations for upgradation and quality improvement of the Education Centres through better infrastructure, as well as intensive training of existing teachers and additional employment of adequate numbers of qualified teachers—all of which will have financial implications.

At the Same Time, Planning for School Education must take into Account the Ecology of Educati®on—The Need to Adjust School Systems to Agro-climatic and Other Local Variations

This requires flexibility with respect to school timings, vacations, teacher recruitment—but without sacrificing quality. Norms for schools must recognise the possibility of regional and local differences as well as the particular requirements of certain communities, such as nomadic groups, tribal communities, short-term migrant households etc.

School Management must be Decentralised as Far as Possible

Decentralisation of the management of schools, combined with community participation, is the most effective instrument for ensuring accountability, improving the day-to-day functioning of schools and allowing for flexible responses to local requirements. Therefore, there should be devolution of authority to local levels, whether to panchayats, Village Education Committees or municipalities. School Management Committees that include representatives of all stakeholders, including parents and teachers, should be empowered to make many decisions. Social audits of schools should be supported and encouraged.

There is a Multiplicity of Management Structures and Government Departments in the Administration of School Education. This Creates Confusion, Unnecessary Replication and Possibly Inconsistent Strategies Across Different Schools. There Must be Greater Co-ordination between Different Departments of Government on School Education Policy, Even While Ensuring More Autonomy to the Local Community in Matters of Day-to-day Management of Schools

Currently schools are run or funded and monitored not only by the Central and State Governments, but also by different departments within State Governments—the Education Department, the Panchayat Department, the Department for Tribal Welfare, the Department for Minority Welfare etc. This creates overlapping and conflicting structures of authority, an excess of bureaucratic tangles, unnecessary replication of some activities (and even replication of enrolment in some cases!), different guidelines and differential standards for acceptable quality and other sorts of confusion. For example, in the rural areas of several states, the local Panchayati Raj Institution (PRI) runs parallel to the SSA run Village Education Committee (VEC). The exact remit of each is not clear and the policy intentions of both become diluted in the process.

It is necessary to make systematic efforts to integrate or at least co-ordinate the activities of these separate management structures. The precise roles and responsibilities of each local level and state level department should be clearly specified, but even more than that, there should be some sort of pressure for these different bodies to work together as far as possible and provide a common and equal schooling. Education policy must be part of the integrated framework of decentralised planning.

In the day-to-day management of schools, it is also necessary to work towards segregating teachers from managers in the school administration. At the same time, as noted above in point I.4, the decentralisation of authority is critical in improving and maintaining the quality of education. Therefore, the local level management of schools, including locally elected bodies, school boards, Village Education Committees, must be allowed a significant degree of autonomy in handling matters relating to their schools, including not only the exact allocation of funds, but also other matters relating to school functioning and monitoring of teachers etc.

There is Need for a National Body to Monitor the Quality of Both Government and Private Schools, to Ensure that Minimum Standards are Met in Terms of Learning Outcomes

Currently there is no systematic and continuous feedback on the actual impact and outcome of various educational schemes and initiatives, or the actual quality of education imparted in schools. There is a strong case for a testing body at the national level for quality assessment of schools. A results-based monitoring framework with due process indicators and outcome indicators needs to be evolved. This should be based on a short list of monitorable criteria. These should include fixed infrastructural requirements, enrolment and attendance, as well as outcome indicators such as learning levels achieved in certain basic areas such as language skills and numeracy etc. Such a process of assessment needs to be applied to all schools—both public and private. However, the testing of students must not involve topics or questions that provide any incentives for rote-learning. The tracking mechanism should ideally be concerned with the profile of skill attainment of each student.

Since school education is largely a state subject, but it is also important to achieve minimum schooling norms at the national level, the institutional framework for this could be at the national level with state subsidiaries. The role of this testing body will simply be to provide information on the results of its assessments, with the State Governments free to act upon this information. The results of such regular tests must be made publicly available in a format accessible to all, including websites.

The monitoring of private schools, in terms of ensuring a transparent admissions process, regulation of fee structures, as well as meeting minimum set standards for quality of teaching and infrastructure, also requires attention. There is currently no exact data on the numbers and enrolment of unrecognised private schools in the country, their fee structure or admissions policy, or their standards of infrastructure and quality. Private schools should become the subject of regulation and inspection within a set framework which is universally applicable.

The System of School Inspection Needs to be Revamped and Revitalised in Most States, with a Greater Role for Local Stakeholders

The current inspection system is overburdened and inadequate, with a small number of inspectors required to cover a large number of schools, often spread over wide physical areas. The solution does not lie in simply expanding the system—rather, we need to develop systems to ensure meaningful monitoring.

NKC recommends that the strategy for the revitalisation of the school inspection system should include the following:

- Local stakeholders should be involved in the monitoring of schools, whether in the form of Village Education Committees, parent associations, or other such bodies.
- The number of inspectors needs to be increased in many states, and they must be provided the facilities to undertake their activities properly, such as transport, communications devices etc.
- The inspectors themselves must be accountable to the stakeholders of the area, through appropriate checks and balances.
- The criteria for inspection, the dates on which inspection of particular schools has taken place and the results should be made publicly available, including by posting on websites.
- The monitoring and inspection of schools must be separated from school administration, as the two functions require completely different orientations.
- The criteria for inspection should include not only infrastructure, facilities and teacher presence but also minimum standards for quality.

The Dignity of School Teaching as a Profession must be Restored, and at the Same Time There should be Transparent Systems for Ensuring Accountability of School Teachers

Teachers constitute the basic foundation of the school education system. However, there is a general decline in morale among school teachers, especially those in primary schools, and consequently it is no longer seen as an attractive profession for qualified young people. Two types of public perceptions, also propagated in the media and among officialdom, contribute to the low morale among school teachers: first, that anyone can teach and no particular pedagogical skills or training are required; second, that in any case most teachers do not work much and are frequently absent from school. While the latter may be the case for a relatively small minority of teachers, most school teachers are committed to their profession even if they have to function under very difficult conditions. However, they are also subject to many other pressures such as political pressure and obligations to perform non-teaching duties, which can prevent them from fulfilling their teaching duties adequately.

It is essential to ensure that qualified teachers are hired and provided with the necessary incentives to enable them to work better. The professional status of teachers should not be diluted, and all drives at recruiting untrained teachers must be checked, although it is important to allow for flexibility in recruitment of teaches for specific subjects such as art, craft and livelihood skills. The use of para-teachers must be treated as a strictly transitional measure until proper schools are established.

The imposition of a wide range of non-teaching duties, such as that of manning poll booths and collecting data for surveys etc., cuts into the available teaching time and also undermines the professional status of teachers. These activities should be shared out among a wider range of public employees or even those hired specifically for the purpose, and the burden of such work on teachers must be reduced. Specifically, unemployed local youth and recently retired people may be considered for such activities as far as possible.

The recruitment of teachers from the locality has many advantages, as they can become accountable to the community, and have added stakes in improving the quality of education in their schools. In cases where local language or dialect is different from the state language, teachers familiar with the local language are likely to make better teachers.

NKC proposes that teachers should be recruited to particular schools as far as possible. At the very minimum, school teachers should be appointed to a particular location for a minimum fixed term of at least five years, since a major problem cited by many teachers in the government school system is that of frequent transfers. (The specific case of attracting teachers to remote and backward areas is considered below under Access.)

There should be increased attempts to improve public recognition of the contribution of school teachers, through various incentives such as more local, state-level and national awards etc.

It is necessary to monitor the emoluments and working conditions of teachers in private schools, which vary substantially, and prevent exploitation of teachers by private school employers as far as possible.

However, in addition to improving the working conditions of teachers, it is also necessary to institute measures to provide greater accountability of school teachers not only to their superiors, but to students, parents and the local community. Currently, any mention of increasing teacher accountability is viewed with hostility and suspicion by teachers themselves. Such an outlook needs to be changed. There is clearly a need for greater accountability of teachers to the community and the school, and this will be facilitated by greater decentralisation of school management to local stakeholders as has been suggested above. This should be accompanied by recognition of the concerns of teachers and allowing them more space to be active in school management and school activities. The actual administrative arrangements whereby this is done should be left to be decided at the state and local level. Systems of self-evaluation and peer evaluation of teachers should be encouraged.

The Training of School Teachers is Extremely Inadequate and also Poorly Managed. Pre-service Training Needs to be Improved and Regulated, While Systems for In-service Training Require Expansion and Major Reform in All States

Both pre-service and in-service teacher training programmes face major problems at present, at the national level and in almost all states. With respect to pre-service training, there is a proliferation of private colleges awarding the B.Ed. degree, and these are inadequately monitored or regulated. A significant proportion of those who receive B.Ed. degrees do so through correspondence or distance learning courses, which involve absolutely no practical exposure. In any case, classroom experience is underplayed in standard B.Ed courses. At the same time, the employment of ad hoc teachers and those without even high school diplomas as teachers in the parallel stream perpetuates the notion that it is not necessary for school teachers to have systematic and prolonged pre-service training.

In-service training shows problems of inadequate quantity, uneven quality, outdated syllabi, and poor management. A very large proportion of school teachers in the country have received no in-service training at all. In any case, many DIETs are currently understaffed, demoralised, and incapable of giving good quality training to teachers. In part, this is because teacher training positions are often occupied by those who have not themselves been school teachers. In many states the administration of DIETs is left to bureaucrats who view this as a punishment posting and have no pedagogical experience. Further, DIETs typically lack adequate infrastructural facilities. Even when in-service training is regularly held, there is no mechanism which can monitor the impact of in service teacher training courses on the subsequent teaching-learning process in the classroom. Most SCERTs themselves hire contract teachers since there are very few qualified and regular teachers and lecturers. These therefore find it difficult to supervise functions at the block level unless their numbers are greatly increased. Funds are needed from the central government for human resource development at this level.

NKC therefore suggests the following for teacher training:

- Institutions providing pre-service teacher training and granting B.Ed degrees should be subject to the same regulatory authority, and there should be adequate monitoring of the training provided by private organisations.
- The budgetary allocation for teacher training needs to be enhanced and made explicit, and central government provisions are required for this.
- There has to be greater flexibility in the modalities of teacher training. Diverse strategies such as greater use of ICT, Visiting Trainers and empowering local trainers who would visit schools should be encouraged.

- State-level teacher training needs to be revamped in most states. The system of DIETs needs to be restructured. In some smaller states, there is a strong case for one state-level institution for teacher training. In other states, the DIETs need to be strengthened and undergo structural changes. The faculty of SCERTs, SIEs and DIETs must be expanded, and include experienced school teachers. The use of contract teachers must be kept to a minimum. In addition, the link between university departments and school teaching needs to be strengthened.
- The administrative hierarchies within DIET and SCERT have to be restructured, so that there is a clear separation of personnel engaged in administrative and academic activities. (This distinction is currently blurred in most states.)
- The teacher training course should not be seen in terms of a finite period of time, but as a process by which the quality of teaching and learning in the classroom can be regularly improved, in a context that fosters an attitude of lifelong learning. Therefore, there should be a mechanism for feedback and subsequent interaction between teachers and the training institutes, especially for pedagogical techniques that are new or require more continuous innovation from the teacher.
- Currently in-service training is offered through pre-determined themes which trivialise the role of personal meaning while upholding requirements dictated by educational reform agendas. Greater freedom of choice would help to increase personal initiative and absorption of training inputs. NKC therefore, suggests the provision of short term in-service courses (in both contact and distance mode) that teachers can choose from. These could include courses developed outside the DIET/SCERT structure, subject to a thorough review of quality.
- In addition to being made more flexible, in-service teaching courses need to be incentivised, possibly by

making attendance at and completion of such courses prerequisites to professional advancement.

- There is need for curricular reform in both pre-service and in-service teacher training. The curriculum should be framed in ways that are directly relevant to teachers and the requirements of particular classroom situations, such as multi grade teaching, special needs of first-generation learners etc. This means that curricula should be framed with greater inputs from teachers themselves, and their practical requirements in the classroom.
- ICT must be incorporated more fully into teacher training programmes, which in turn leads to ICT being used more freely in the classroom.
- It is necessary to develop content for and access to open educational resources for teacher training.

It is Important to Develop and Nurture Leadership for Managing Schools

Even talented individuals who could be suitable for the tasks of school management need to be trained for this purpose. Such capacity building would create a pool of potential principals or heads. There are several ways in which this can be done. State Governments could assign such training to existing institutions such as SCERTs or SIEs, leveraging the expertise available in Navodaya Vidyalayas, Kendriya Vidyalayas, other government schools and private schools. Such training programmes, as well as re-training programmes for existing principals, could also seek the expertise of specialists in management education. Also, individual mentoring programmes for school leaders could be evolved.

The Possibility of Greater Exchange between Schools, Including Mentoring of One School by Another should be Allowed and Encouraged

The current system creates many distinctions and prevents interaction between schools. There is a need to constitute mechanisms of exchange and interaction between students and teachers of different schools. In addition, schools that wish to do so should be allowed to exercise the option of being 'mentored' by another school to improve facilities and teaching methods.

Curriculum Reform Remains an Important Issue in Almost All Schools. School Education must be Made More Relevant to the Lives of Children. There is Need to Move Away from Rote-learning to Understanding Concepts, Good Comprehension and Communication Skills and Learning How to Access Knowledge Independently

Successive Commissions and Committees set up by the government have emphasised the need to make the curriculum more interesting, relevant, creative and useful for students. The National Curriculum Framework 2005 also clearly articulated such an approach. Nevertheless it appears that in a majority of schools across the country, a significant emphasis on rote-learning and memorising facts remains the norm. Also, there is evidence of children being overburdened with too much detail and an excess of scholastic requirements at the elementary level.

It is important to orient students towards independent and continuous learning. This makes it essential to make greater efforts to change the attitude to learning and knowledge. It has been noted in several states that learning results have improved considerably upon providing inputs for communication and comprehension in language and basic mathematical skills using activity-based and imaginative pedagogical strategies. The focus of primary schooling in particular must be on good language and communication skills, basic foundation maths and inculcation of self-learning and critical examination through innovative teaching methods. For language teaching in particular, there should be much greater emphasis on communication skills at a practical level.

It is also important to ensure that the curriculum contains locally relevant content that children can relate to their own lives. For example, in certain parts of the country (such as, but not only, the Northeast) the curriculum at both primary and secondary levels could also include training in disaster management, especially for floods, while in other parts of the country responses to earthquakes may be more relevant. In rural areas, horticulture and pisciculture techniques should be included in the syllabus. Co-curricular reading material should be propagated, such as children's books with local stories and histories to strengthen the linkages between school and home.

To make secondary school education more relevant, and also address the problem of drop outs, NKC recommends the setting up of Livelihood Centres in secondary schools that would impart practical employable skills and provide career counselling to students. All school children should be encouraged to be involved in some practical activities that require working with the hands. These activities should not be treated as catering to a parallel stream, but should be provided to all students and integrated with the overall syllabus. Once again, links with the Skill Development Mission should be developed wherever possible.

Changes in the Examination System are Required, Especially at Board Level but also Earlier, to Ensure that the Pressure for Rote-learning is Reduced

The current over-emphasis on details, memorising of facts and similar abilities rather than on understanding and accessing knowledge independently is reflected in the pattern of examinations. Board examinations in which marks are awarded based on the ability to recall lots of details or on rapidity of response or on the ability to do large numbers of sums in a limited period through practice in pattern recognition, are not sufficiently discriminatory and may end up providing misleading results. They also put pressure on schools to ensure that memory and pattern recognition skills are developed at the expense of genuine understanding.

This is also reflected in the pattern of annual examinations which many schools continue to run even in junior classes such as Class III and Class V. Performance in such examinations then becomes the basis for choosing students who will be eligible for scholarships or gain entrance to Navodaya Vidyalayas and similar schools. Forcing children to undergo a large number of examinations in different subjects, with an emphasis on memory rather than comprehension, must be discouraged at the primary level.

For curriculum reform to be successful, it is necessary to make major changes in the examination system. This applies equally to some of the national school boards (such as CBSE) and the state-level boards. It is also crucial to push for such reform in the annual examinations held by schools, where the testing must be focused on language and comprehension, numeric and quantitative skills, and ability to use knowledge creatively.

New Technologies, Especially but Not Only ICT, should be Used as Much as Possible to Reduce Costs, Enable More Effective Use of Resources, and Provide Wider Exposure to Students and Teachers

The use of ICT as a teaching and learning device needs to be more firmly incorporated into the classroom. Both teachers and students need to be far more familiar with ICT, and get practical experience of web based research. Therefore ICT should be made more accessible to teachers, students and administration for learning, training, research, administration, management, monitoring etc. This requires the provision of more facilities such as computers as well as connectivity and broadband facilities. Computer-aided learning also requires training of teachers and other staff in order to make the best use of the technology.

There is Need for a Web-based Portal for Teachers to Exchange Ideas, Information and Experiences

A forum for teachers needs to be developed where they may interact, share experiences and ideas. This needs to be incorporated into teacher training programmes, and also provided generally for in-service teachers. A web-based teachers' portal can play an important role as such a networking forum.

Access

Special Strategies are Required to Ensure Greater Access to Schools in Backward Regions, Remote Locations and Difficult Terrains

There is a tremendous shortage of teachers and also great difficulty in ensuring minimum schooling infrastructure in some areas that have been historically deprived or have difficult topographical conditions. Distance and difficulty of physical access are important reasons for school drop out, especially in such areas. Sometimes it is also the case that such areas are inhabited by particular communities with their own language or dialect that is different from the state language. In order to ensure access to schools for children in such areas, special measures must be taken.

NKC recommends the following measures for such areas:

- Financial norms for schools in such locations must be different from those in more accessible areas, as they will require additional resource allocation based on particular conditions.
- Special incentives, including a financial incentive (such as a "hardship bonus") need to be provided for teachers to take up jobs in such areas. Two different models may be considered—one based on recruiting local teachers on a permanent basis for a job in a particular school without transfer; and another based on a transfer policy that divides locations into hard/middle/easy categories and allows teachers to rotate among them at specified intervals. Ideally, there should be at least one local teacher and one non-local teacher to ensure some variation, local acceptability and quality.
- Residential arrangements must be made for teachers in such locations, by providing quarters next to or near the school. The cost of building such quarters should be factored into the costs of the school building.
- There are some geographical zones especially in mountainous regions, that are plagued by unique

problems due to vast tracts of land, difficult topography, and a sparse and nomadic population. In such areas, well equipped residential schools should be set up instead of insisting on a school in every habitation. These schools must be equipped to look into the needs of very young children living away from their families.

Measures are Required to Ensure Greater Enrolment and Retention of Girl Students

The high drop out rate of girls especially from Class V onwards is a matter of great concern. One major reason, as noted above, is the sheer lack of secondary schools nearby, as parents are reluctant to send girls to travel long distances to school. However, social conditioning and other constraints also play a role. Some policies to address this include:

- Special incentives for girls in secondary education where these are required (they are not required everywhere), in addition to free textbooks and uniforms, such as bicycles.
- Girls-only schools especially in particular areas.
- An enhanced scholarship scheme especially for girls, with particular emphasis on girls from socially deprived groups.
- The need for separate and functional toilets for girls in all schools, with access to water, is very important, especially but not exclusively in urban areas.

Language Issues must be Explicitly Taken on Board in Designing School Curricula and Methods of Pedagogy

Language has been found to be a highly alienating factor in the education of many school children, particularly amongst minorities, tribal communities with languages without a script, as well as linguistic minorities in most states. Many children resent the imposition of the state language as the medium of instruction, or as second language in school.

More teachers for teaching minority languages must be appointed in government schools to increase the intake of children from minority language communities. Qualified teachers from the local community and therefore speaking the same language must be recruited on a larger scale, as a means of encouraging retention amongst those who feel marginalised, as well as a means of bringing greater community control in the school. This would also act as a boost to confidence, and provide role models to students from disadvantaged backgrounds.

The Teaching of English should be Introduced along with the First Language, Starting from Class I in School

Proficiency in English is widely perceived as an important avenue for employment and upward mobility, which also greatly facilitates the pursuit of higher education. The incorporation of English into the curriculum, through the introduction of English as a language in Class I and the teaching of one other subject in English medium in later classes, requires pedagogical changes to contextualise language learning, increasing the availability of English language teachers and those who can teach at least one subject in English, as well as bilingual and supplementary teaching materials.

At the same time, school education must commit to promoting multi-linguality, given the multilingual nature of our country.

There is Need to Re-orient Official Strategies for Ensuring Better Access of Muslim Children to Schooling

Areas with Muslim majority population have tended to be overlooked in the implementation of government educational schemes. In addition, with a few exceptions, there has been less private initiative in this regard. As a consequence, Muslims as a community, have access to fewer government schools, girls schools, and higher educational institutions.

It is important to rectify this gap and ensure adequate public expenditure to ensure that the physical and social infrastructure for schooling is made available. This means that the government should have a minority component in all its school development schemes and budget outlays, which should be in proportion to the minority population.

The strategy cannot be based solely on more public resources provided to madrasas for their modernisation, as according to the Sachar Committee Report, 96 per cent of Muslim children do not attend madrasas for schooling. Indeed, if the modernisation of madrasa education is the only policy for increasing access for Muslim school children to modernised education, it will only result in their being further isolated.

It is important to ensure that children from all minorities and socially deprived groups are not discriminated against in the process of attending school. This must be an active and concerted campaign, in which syllabi and curriculum are checked to avoid prejudice, teachers are sensitised and instances of discrimination are punished. This also requires grievance redressal mechanisms at the school level and also at higher levels.

The Access of Children from Scheduled Tribes Requires more Flexible and Sensitive Schooling Strategies

Tribal children face problems of inadequate geographical access, discrimination at school and issues of language, which have been discussed earlier but are especially relevant in these cases. Tribal students have to compete with SC students, often at a disadvantage to the former. All of these must be addressed at the local level as well as at the district and state level.

Every state should have an education policy for tribal and minority education, with a long term vision of eventual integration into the mainstream.

Rather than setting up separate schools for those who have dropped out because they felt discriminated against, teachers should be better sensitised to the needs of students from such communities, as well as the particular needs of first generation learners.

The issue of language is particularly important in areas with tribal population, and care must be taken to find and train teachers who can deal with children in their own language, rather than forcing them to adjust to the regional language.

Education of SC Children must be a Priority, but with the Required Flexibility and Avoidance of Discrimination

The points made earlier with respect to discrimination are especially valid also for SC children, and must be addressed in similar ways.

In addition, scholarships should be increased and provided to much larger numbers of Dalit children, along with other provisions such as free textbooks up to Class X and other incentives.

Children of Seasonal Migrants Require Special Conditions and Efforts to Ensure Continuous Access to Schooling

Seasonal and short-term migration is a major cause for early drop outs and non enrolment. In order to ensure that such children have access to a quality and complete education, their economic insecurity has to be taken into account while formulating educational schemes. Tent schools and mobile schools must be made a part of the urban landscape for migrant children, while rural schools also have to be made aware of the need to admit migrant children. This requires a significant change in the way that school admissions and enrolment are carried out, as well as greater sensitivity, flexibility and effort on the part of the school administration, all of which require hard and soft resources. It is necessary to identify good practices in this regard which can serve as a model to be emulated elsewhere.

Labouring Children Require Incentives and Bridge Courses

Some sort of monetary stipend may have to be paid to labouring children to bring them into schools. In addition, synergies must be created with NREGA to look into school education concerns of labouring children. Pre-school systems like balwadis and anganwadis must be strengthened, so that a school going habit can be ingrained, as well as providing a space for small children to be cared for, while their elder siblings may go to school.

Alternative Centres for Education must be utilised specifically to provide bridge courses aimed at different age groups and classes for drop outs. However, the use of Alternative Centres for Education must be no more than in a transition capacity. AIE should not become the only option for access to poor school children for a school education.

Study Centres must be provided for first generation learners and seasonal migrants as a space which is more conducive to learning than what may be available at home. These may also be used as community centres, libraries etc.

The Needs of Physically Disadvantaged Children, as Well as Teachers, have to be Factored in More thoroughly in Provisions for School Education

The goal in all schools should be inclusive education, which means that all systems must be oriented to allow the greatest possible access to children with different needs and abilities. This requires substantial changes in both infrastructure and pedagogical methods. School buildings must have provisions for access and navigation for the visually impaired, the physically handicapped etc. Teachers must be trained, sensitised and empowered to deal with children with different abilities in the classroom situation.

While this is the ultimate goal, it must also be recognised that current schooling patterns are not always conducive to bringing out the full potential of physically disadvantaged children, and therefore, there is still a case for special schools. There is a perception that government mechanisms may not be best suited to provide sustained and sympathetic support for learners with special needs and severely disabled children (such as the blind). In this context, it may be better to identify appropriate and willing institutions outside the government who may become partners.

General Observations

The most important shortening in the report is that it ignores financial implications. It is simply a well written essay.

5

Secondary Education; Universalizing Opportunity: World Bank Report, 2009

INTRODUCTION

This chapter includes the major observations and recommendations made in a report published by Human Development Unit-South Asian Region, World Bank.

The overall picture which emerges is that the steady historical expansion of secondary education is poised to accelerate over the next decade. Aggressive efforts are needed to address both supply-and demand-side constraints to make this potential expansion a realistic possibility, particularly for certain groups (girls, poor, STs, SCs, Muslims) whose respective enrollment rates in secondary education are far below country averages. These efforts are inextricably linked to activities to improve the quality of elementary and secondary education, in order to make that access meaningful for students and society as a whole.

WHY INVEST IN SECONDARY EDUCATION IN INDIA?

This includes the views of Kin Bing Wu and Amir Dar of World Bank.

Secondary Education in India is essential foundation for democratic citizenship. The experience of post-World War II Germany and Japan in advancing democracy and peace testifies to the constructive and transformational power of education. Secondary education in the humanities and social sciences raises an individual's capacity for social and political discourse and enhance participation in political and civic affairs (World Bank, 2005a). Finally, while primary education takes place within relatively homogenous communities, secondarv schools typically enroll more students with greater diversity given their larger catchment areas, which creates greater opportunities to foster citizenship and communal tolerance.

International Competitiveness

Expansion of higher education goal of the next ten years, will only be possible if secondary education expands first (Table 5.1, Fig. 5.1 and Fig. 5.2).

Table 5.1: Secondary Gross Enrollment Rates by Country

Country	*GDP/Capita (US$)*	*Secondary GER (%)*
India	720	52
Bangladesh	470	52
Brazil	3,460	110
China	1,740	81
Indonesia	1,280	61
Kenya	530	48
Moldova	690	74
Mexico	7,310	79
Nicaragua	910	61
Pakistan	690	44
Peru	2,610	90

Conclusion

The rationale for public investment in secondary education lies in its contribution to economic growth, demonstrated high social benefits, positive impact on equity, ability to overcome education market failures and household misperceptions of the value of secondary education, preparation for higher education and generation of knowledge, and, finally, its contribution to democratic citizenship and social cohesion.

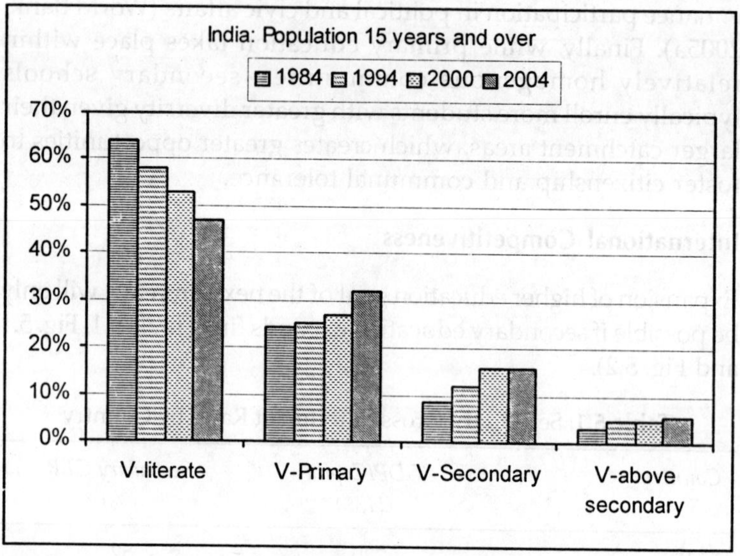

Fig. 5.1: India's "Stock of Skills".

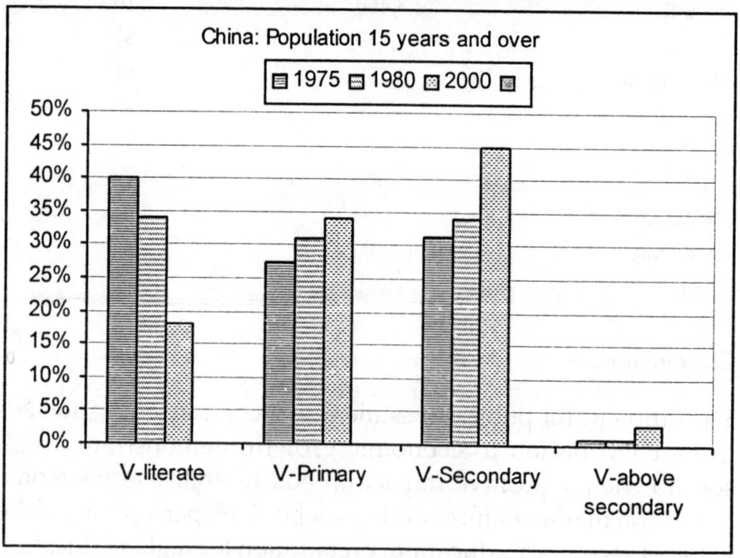

Fig. 5.2: China's "Stock of Skills".

SYSTEM DESCRIPTION

- While enrolments have increased at all levels, secondary education enrolment growth has lagged that of elementary education......
  - Elementary Education (Grades 1-7/8): ~ 94 per cent of the 6-13-year-olds in school (2005)
  - Secondary and senior secondary education (Grades 9-12): rising but enrolment ratio still under 40 per cent (2003)
  - Tertiary education enrolment ratio is about 10 percent.
- Unlike elementary education where the centre and states both play a important role in financing and setting standards, at the secondary level, states decide on their own educational systems and policies within a national framework.
- While there is substantial variation across states (see below), India's public spending on the secondary sub-sector is about 1.2 per cent of GDP (US$4.1 billion).
- India has a long tradition of partnership between the public and private sectors in secondary education. There are four types of schools:
  - government—established by state governments (as well as some centrally established institutions);
  - local body-established by elected local government bodies;
  - aided schools-private schools that receive state government grants-in-aid; and private unaided schools.
- Most of the growth of secondary schools in the private sector in the last two decades has occurred among unaided schools (25% of schools). About 60 per cent of schools are now aided or unaided. Enrolments follow roughly the same pattern.

KEY CHALLENGES

- While demand for secondary school graduates has increased, supply has not kept pace, and GoI is mulling over suggestions to universalize secondary education But significant challenges need to be addressed......

Access

- While over 33 million enrolled, enrollment rates are still low (38%)
- Wide gender gap remains—only one third of students are girls
- Rich/poor, urban/rural, and minority/non-minority gaps have not narrowed significantly over time.

SOCIAL DIVIDE MOST PROMINENT IN SECONDARY EDUCATION—DIFFERENTIAL ACCESS BETWEEN TOP AND BOTTOM QUINTILES ACROSS STATES

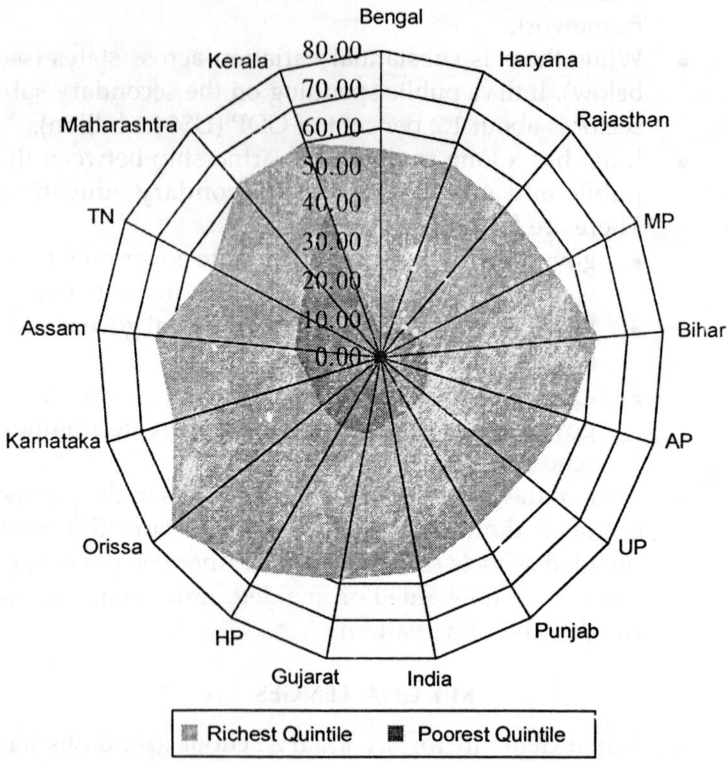

Fig. 5.3

INTERNATIONAL COMPARISONS

As a result, India lags behind other comparator countries—only 17 per cent of Indians over age 25 have had some secondary education, compared with 36 per cent in China, 17 per cent in Sub-Saharan Africa, and 28 per cent in the world at large, and India's enrolment ratio in secondary education is lower than would be predicted by its per capita income level.

Possible Reasons for Low Access

- Low transition rates-out of 100 entering Grade 1 less than 50 make it to secondary level.
- Demand-side factors: high direct and opportunity costs of schooling, and lack of information on the benefits of secondary education and value of girls education.
- Supply-side factors: lack of adequate infrastructure (e.g. over 1/3rdof villages have schools beyond 5 kms.), inadequate incentives for private sector to expand, and inflexible delivery system (few second chances).

Quality

- There is no regular system of benchmarking students comparatively with other countries or even across states.
- Tests of a sample of students in Grades 9 and 11 (in Raj. And Orissa) using the mathematics test items developed under the Third International Mathematics and Science Study (TIMSS) found low achievement.

Possible Reasons for Low Achievement

- Poor quality and low student achievement at the elementary levels
- Too much emphasis on rote learning
- Insufficient development of conceptual understanding and higher order thinking
- Insufficient quality assurance and accountability
- Low capacity in institutions for teacher pre-service and in-service training.

Should India Invest More in Secondary Education?

Yes...there are clear economic reasons.

- Marginal rates of return are high in secondary education and among women, and increasing in upper secondary and tertiary education
- There is increasing demand for secondary school graduates
- Social benefits from lower total fertility rates, better health, and intergenerational mobility, particularly when women are better educated.

Rates of Return to Education

See Fig: 5.5.

Relative Demand and Supply: Secondary Education

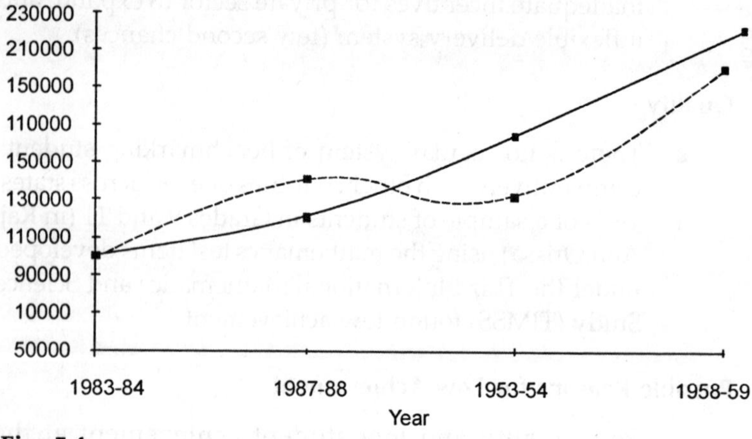

Fig.: 5.4

How should the Expansion in Secondary Education Take Place—Options

Access

- Encouraging the private sector is critical. Surveys from two states show that private school are more cost-

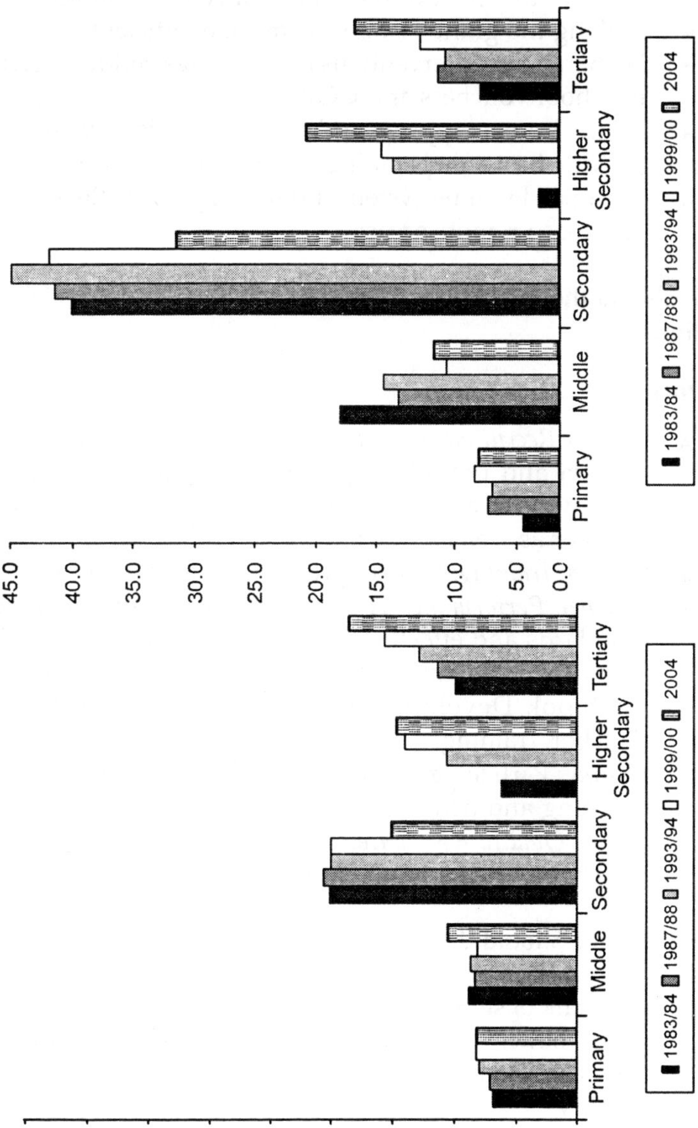
45.0
40.0
35.0
30.0
25.0
20.0
15.0
10.0
5.0
0.0
Primary
Middle
Secondary
Higher Secondary
Tertiary
1983/84
1987/88
1993/94
1999/00
2004

Fig. 5.5

effective—students do not perform worse than public schools students even though unit costs are lower
- Making the grant-in-aid system more efficient
- Demand-side interventions to encourage children to go to school-vouchers and CCTs
- Use school mapping and school facility audits to provide basis for planning and resource allocation
- Use open learning system and ICT to provide flexibility and reach remote areas;

How should the Expansion in Secondary Education Take Place-Options

Quality

- *Teacher Recruitment and Management*: Improve selection criteria and provide appropriate incentives; Flexible deployment and clear transfer policy (criteria for transfer as well as well as a cap on turn-over)
- *Teacher Training*: Reform pre-Service and In-Service
- *Teacher Performance Assessment*: Clear performance standards and effective assessment systems
- *Curriculum Reform*: Alignment of NCF with Syllabus, Textbook Development, Student Assessment and Teacher Training.
- *Testing*: Participate in international studies for capacity building and benchmarking
- *School Quality Assurance*: Strengthen academic support to schools and set up quality assurance.

At What Pace Should the Expansion Take Place

- Any talk of significant expansion at the secondary level only makes sense when the elementary education agenda is complete—ensuring universal retention and quality.
- Under a realistic scenario of 5 per cent *annual* reduction in repetition and dropout rates at the elementary level—GER at sec. level would be 75 per cent and senior sec.

at 60 per cent by 2020. And this does not take into account the importance of improving quality at the sec. level.

- Given this, the focus should not be on universalization at the sec. level—but on enhancing access gradually while major emphasis is placed on improving quality.

How Much will it Cost?

Under the scenario presented above, and assuming annual GDP growth rates of 7 per cent, an investment of an additional 0.2-0.3 percent of GDP per year is likely to achieve these realistic targets.

Summary

Some Facts

- 40 million children were enrolled in secondary school in 2008. The majority of them were boys, children from the urban areas, and those who belonged to the wealthier segments of the population.
- Enrollment varies greatly between states, from 92 per cent in Kerala, 44 per cent in Tamil Nadu, 22 per cent in Bihar, and 4 per cent in Jharkhand. 37 per cent of secondary students fail, and 11 per cent dropout before exam.
- There are 3 National Boards and 34 State and Union Territory Boards, with their own curriculum and certifying examinations.
- 75 per cent of public funding for secondary schools comes from states. Less than 10 per cent of this is for investment. While recurrent financing, mainly for teacher salaries, has been stable, the financing of new investments has declined.
- 60 per cent of the secondary school system is privately managed—through unaided and aided private schools. Private unaided schools provide 30 per cent of total secondary enrollment nationwide (2004-05), up from

15 per cent in 1993-94. Their dramatic growth reveals the demand for secondary schooling and the willingness and capacity of households to pay for it. This however leads to the increasing inequality as poorer households cannot afford to pay both the direct and opportunity costs of their children's secondary education.

- On average, government school teachers earn 3 times more than their counterparts in private schools.
- The quality of schooling as measured in students' cognitive skills is more important than the number of years of schooling in determining students' future incomes. Once quality is established, years of schooling matter. Just increasing years of schooling does not appear to be worthwhile.
- Unfortunately, small scale standardized assessments of student achievement suggest that the quality of instruction and learning for the large majority of students is very low.
- Schools determine some 50 per cent of student achievement. Factors that determine the quality of education include: the quality of teachers; the curricula and teaching processes; quality and availability of learning materials—textbooks and ICTs. However, the availability of ICTs is very limited, and teachers' pre-service education suffers from poor standards, there is a shortage of candidates with the necessary attributes, insufficient objectivity and political interference in hiring, and a high frequency of court cases.

Recommendations

- *Construct public schools,* especially in rural areas where private suppliers are unlikely to venture;
- *Pilot innovative public-private partnership models* which utilize unused capacity in private schools; PPP does not mean privatization;
- *Introduce double-shift teaching* in urban schools;

- *Expand use of open learning and new technologies,* particularly for out-of-school youth and those who want a "second chance";
- *Invest in curriculum revision,* progressive pedagogy, technology and examination reforms;
- *Invest in ICTs,* so that students can take greater control of their learning and skills acquisition from sources other than the teacher and textbook;
- *Develop and apply clear teacher performance standards, and decentralize teacher recruitment to district or school level,* initially on a contractual basis (no automatic tenure). Transfers to be within district only;
- *Increase schools' autonomy and parental involvement;*
- *Reform Grant-in-Aid System* to make public financing conditional on achieving performance standards, and/ or finance on a per student (or even per graduate) basis;
- *Provide financial and in-kind assistance for poor and disadvantaged students;*
- *Provide financial incentives and technical support for states* to further align their curricula and Board exams with National Curriculum Framework 2005.

6

National Knowledge Commission (2006)
Major Observations and Recommendations

Appointment of the Commission

On June 13, 2005, the Prime Minister of India, Dr. Manmohan Singh constituted the National Knowledge Commission (NKC) as a think-tank to advise the Prime Minister's Office (PMO) on policy related to education, research institutes and reforms needed to make India competitive in the knowledge economy.

Members of the NKC

The National Knowledge Commission (NKC) consists of the following seven members:

1. Sam Pitroda, Chairman
2. Ashok Ganguly, Corporate Leader
3. Nandan Nilekani, Infosys
4. Dr. Deepak Nayyar, Former Vice-Chancellor, University of Delhi
5. Dr. Jayati Ghosh, Economist at Jawaharlal Nehru University
6. Dr. Sujatha Ramadorai, TIFR
7. Dr. P. Balaram, Indian Institute of Science, Bangalore

The Terms of Reference of the NKC:

1. "Build excellence in the educational system to meet the knowledge challenges of the 21st century and increase India's competitive advantage in fields of knowledge.
2. Promote creation of knowledge in science and technology laboratories.

3. Improve the management of institutions engaged in Intellectual Property Rights.
4. Promote knowledge applications in Agriculture and Industry.
5. Promote the use of knowledge capabilities in making government an effective, transparent and accountable service provider to the citizen and promote widespread sharing of knowledge to maximise public benefit".

The secretariat is headed by an Executive Director and consists of about 8-9 research associates. It has four advisers to advise the Commission on different issues. The Secretariat of the Commission is located at Chanakyapuri, New Delhi.

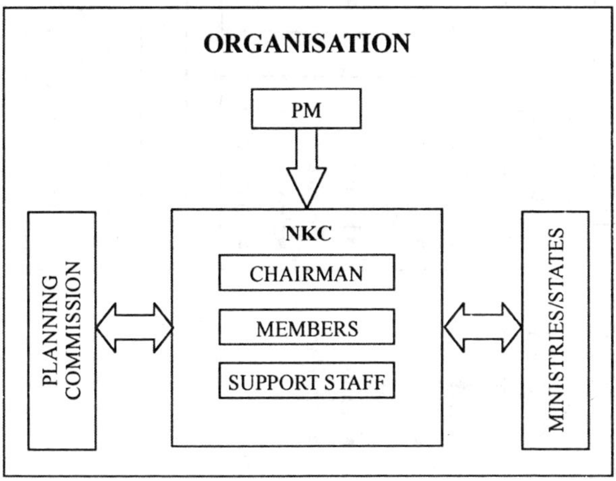

OVERSIGHT MECHANISM

- A national steering group for the NKC headed by the PM, includes Ministers of
  - Agriculture
  - HRD
  - S&T
  - Commerce
  - IT
  - Planning

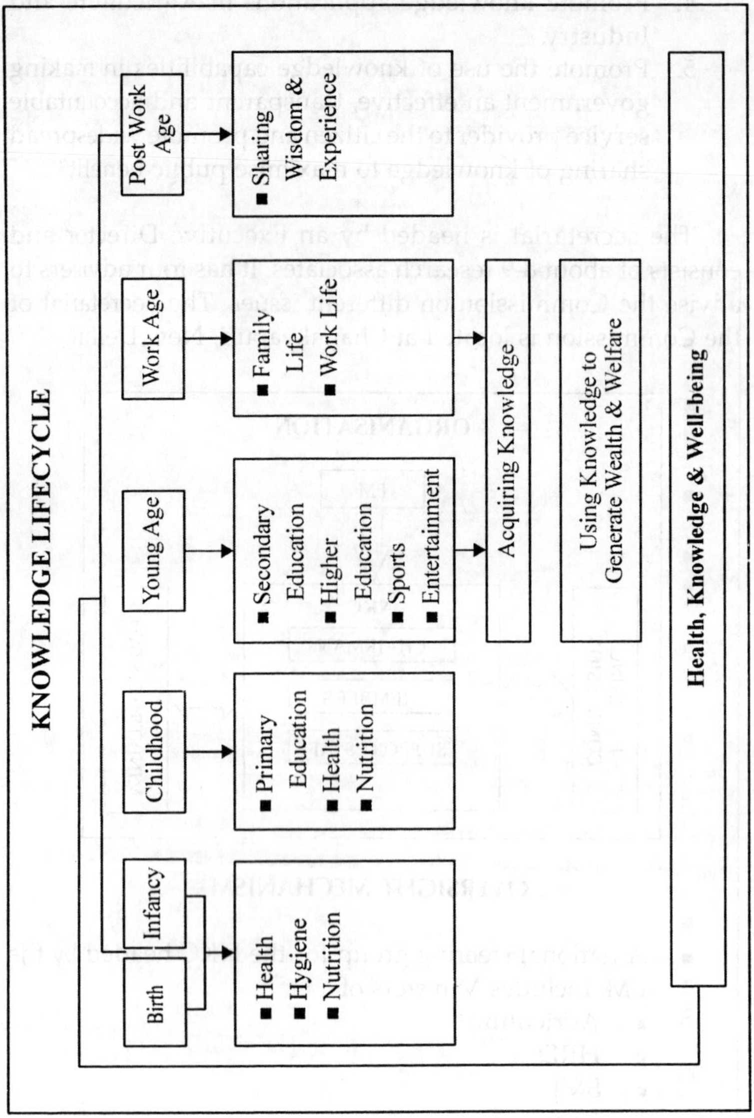
KNOWLEDGE LIFECYCLE
Birth
Infancy
Childhood
Young Age
Work Age
Post Work Age
■ Health ■ Hygiene ■ Nutrition
■ Primary Education ■ Health ■ Nutrition
■ Secondary Education ■ Higher Education ■ Sports ■ Entertainment
■ Family Life ■ Work Life
■ Sharing Wisdom & Experience
Acquiring Knowledge
Using Knowledge to Generate Wealth & Welfare
Health, Knowledge & Well-being

KNOWLEDGE PENTAGON

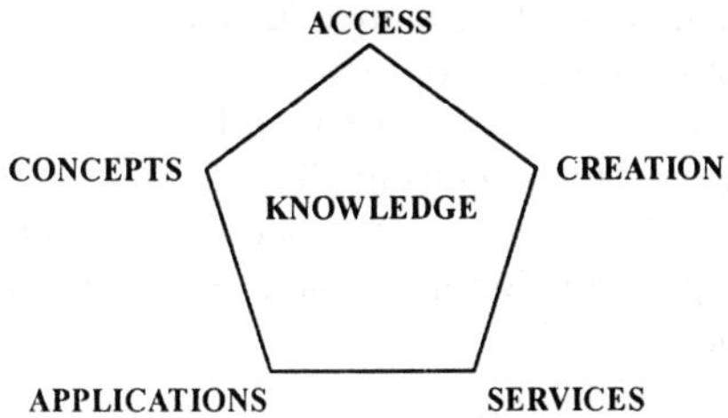

ACTIONS – GENERAL

- Link knowledge initiatives to expedite the process of meeting basic human needs
- Encourage innovations and entrepreneurship at all levels
- Use knowledge to fuel growth in agriculture, manufacturing and services
- Restructure existing institutions to respond to knowledge needs of tomorrow
- Create new institutions to respond to the needs of tomorrow
- Empower people and institutions to participate in the knowledge economy
- Encourage knowledge sharing forums and discussion groups in schools, colleges, libraries, R & D institutions, youth groups, etc.
- Institute district, state, and central awards to recognise people for
    - Innovations
    - Entrepreneurship
    - Education
    - Health
- Motivate, mobilise, support and encourage existing and new knowledge initiatives at various levels in the country
- Help build knowledge infrastructure and institutions
- Focus on knowledge for
    - Individual advancement
    - National development
    - Security
- Use knowledge to leverage new economic opportunities from globalisation

(*Contd.*)

Scaling Excellence in Education and Research

- Extensive access to quality educational resources
  - For faculty development
  - Direct education (formal and non-formal)
  - Meet hr (kw) needs in all sectors
- Quality educational and research interactions
- Global participation in research and education
  - Sharing
  - Benchmarking

Observations and Recommendations of the Commission (2006)

The observations and recommendations of the Commission are contained in the following letters addressed by the Chairman of the Commission to the Prime Minister.

1. Right to Education — Letter dated October 23, 2006
2. Higher Education — Letter dated November 29, 2006
3. Vocational Education — Letter dated December 1, 2006

RIGHT TO EDUCATION

Observations

The National Knowledge Commission has been examining a range of issues related to school education, including access, quality and other issues. We believe that providing universal access to quality school education is a cornerstone of development and a minimum necessary condition for any progress towards making India a knowledge society. We are in the process of extensive consultations and will make detailed recommendations on various issues relating to school education at a later date.

However, at this point we would like to respond specifically to the recent initiative of the central government of sending a model Right to Education Bill to the Secretaries of State Education Departments, with incentives for the state governments to enact this bill. We have perused the bill and consulted with a wide range of experts and educationists. We feel that the model bill is flawed for a number of reasons, and most importantly that such legislation must be enforced by the central government following upon the commitment made in the Constitutional Amendment Article 21A. We recognise that there may be concerns about federalism, since school education is dominantly the responsibility of the state governments at present.

Recommendations/Proposals

However, we feel that this matter can be resolved through appropriate central legislation which takes into account the following proposals:

1. *Central Legislation*: Legislation at the national level is required to affirm the Right to Education, which is a fundamental right mandated by Article 21A. Since it cannot be dependent upon which state a citizen is resident in, a model bill sent to be enacted individually by State Governments is not adequate to meet the constitutional responsibilities of the Government of India. Therefore, a central legislation should be enacted along the lines of the Panchayati Raj (Amendment) Act, requiring the states to enact Right to Education Bills within a specified time period, and with the primary financial responsibility for this resting with the central government.

2. *Financial Commitment*: The Central Government must provide the bulk of the additional funds required to ensure the Right to Education. Therefore there must be financial provision in the central legislation, requiring the central government to share the revenues of the Prarambhik Shiksha Kosh with state governments and to provide additional resources as required to meet the requirement of ensuring the right to education for all children. Estimates for the additional resources required to achieve the goal of universal elementary education currently range from 0.8 per cent to 2.5 per cent of GDP, depending on the criteria used. However, the required financial resources are likely to be at the lower end of these estimates, since there is already close to universal provision in several states and there

has been recent progress in providing more access through the Sarva Shiksha Abhiyan in other states.

3. *Time Frame*: The state-level legislation should specify the period within which universal education of reasonable quality is sought to be achieved, preferably within three years. The model bill does not provide any time frame for adoption and implementation of the provisions.

4. *Schedule of Norms and Standards*: To ensure a minimum quality of education, it is important to have a schedule of norms for all schools to follow. The model bill does not have such a schedule of norms, and there is no specification of the minimum quality of education that schools should provide. There is only a reference to 'equitable quality' without defining the parameters of quality. While ensuring quality is a complex matter, certain norms regarding infrastructure, number of teachers per school and per student, teaching methods and other facilities, etc. must be adhered to as necessary conditions.

5. *Specification for Teachers*: Since teachers are critical in ensuring the quality of education, laying down well-defined but flexible norms for the minimum qualifications of teachers is particularly important. The model bill has no specification of a teacher, or the qualifications and in-service training needed for the position. A teacher is only defined as a person who teaches in the classroom. However, here too it is necessary to specify norms for teacher qualification and training.

6. *Justifiability*: Any right, including the Right to Education, is only meaningful if it is justifiable. However, in the model bill sent to state governments, the onus is placed on parents/guardians of the child. The responsibility of the Government, at different levels, must be recognised and made justifiable. The example of the National Rural Employment Guarantee Act (NREGA) could be used in this context.

7. *Redressal Mechanism*: To ensure justifiability, a redressal mechanism should be outlined and an appropriate procedure must be set in place for students or parents in case the right is not upheld.

8. *Universal Schooling*: School education must be provided to all, which necessarily also requires that children of the

disadvantaged, landless and minority communities must also be integrated, along with children with disabilities or special needs. This requires there should be no distinction made in terms of the type of schooling provided within the government system, for children from different social, economic and cultural backgrounds. The model bill has the potential of creating a parallel and discriminatory system of schooling which can result in stratification of the education system for children from disadvantaged communities and backgrounds, because it requires only provision of non-formal education in such cases, rather than mandating the provision of regular schooling. Obviously, in all cases, the school system should be flexible enough to cater to particular needs of students.

We will be happy to provide detailed explanations on the points mentioned above. The National Knowledge Commission is continuing to consult with stakeholders and examine other issues in relation to school education. We are focussing in particular on the questions of bow to ensure better quality across the board; the institutional structures and forms of control by local communities that could contribute to improved quality of schooling; issues related to common schooling and neighbourhood schools; ensuring adequate quantity and quality of school teachers, especially in specified areas; etc. We will submit a broader set of recommendations on school education in the near future.

HIGHER EDUCATION

Observations

Higher education has made a significant contribution to economic development, social progress and political democracy in independent India. But there is serious cause for concern at this juncture. The proportion of our population, in the relevant age group, that enters the world of higher education is about 7 per cent. The opportunities for higher education in terms of the number of places in universities are simply not adequate in relation to our needs. Large segments of our population just do not have access to higher education. What is more, the quality of higher education in most of our universities leaves much to be desired.

At the outset, we would also like to stress that foundations are critical. We believe that an emphasis on expansion and reform of our school system is necessary to ensure that every child has an equal opportunity to enter the world of higher education.

The NKC has engaged in formal and informal consultations on this subject with a wide range of people in the world of higher education. In addition, we consulted concerned people in parliament, government, civil society and industry. The concerns about the higher education system are widely shared. There was a clear, almost unanimous, view that higher education needs a systematic overhaul, so that we can educate much larger numbers without diluting academic standards. Indeed, this is essential because the transformation of economy and society in the twenty-first century would depend, in significant part, on the spread and the quality of education among our people, particularly in the sphere of higher education. And it is only an inclusive society that can provide the foundations for a knowledge society.

The objectives of reform and change in our higher education system, as you have often stressed, must be expansion, excellence and inclusion. We recognise that meaningful reform of the higher education system, with a long-term perspective, is both complex and difficult. Yet, it is imperative. Our analysis, diagnosis and prescriptions are set out in a detailed note on higher education which is attached. In this letter, we simply highlight our prescriptions.

Recommendations

A. Expansion

1. *Create Many More Universities*: The higher education system needs a massive expansion of opportunities, to around 1500 universities nationwide, that would enable India to attain

a gross enrolment ratio of at least 15 per cent by 2015. The focus would have to be on new universities, but some clusters of affiliated colleges could also become universities. Such expansion would require major changes in the structure of regulation.

2. *Change the System of Regulation for Higher Education*: The present regulatory system in higher education is flawed in some important respects. The barriers to entry are too high. The system cf authorising entry is cumbersome. There is a multiplicity of regulatory agencies where mandates are both confusing and overlapping. The system, as a whole, is over-regulated but under-governed. We believe that there is a clear need to establish an Independent Regulatory Authority for Higher Education (IRAHE). The IRAHE must be at an arm's-length from the government and independent of all stakeholders including the concerned Ministries of the Government.

- The IRAHE would have to be established by an Act of Parliament, and would be responsible for setting the criteria and deciding on entry.
- It would be the only agency that would be authorised to accord degree granting power to higher education institutions.
- It would be responsible for monitoring standards and settling disputes.
- It would apply exactly the same norms to public and private institutions, just as it would apply the same norms to domestic and international institutions.
- It would be the authority for licensing accreditation agencies.
- The role of the UGC would be re-defined to focus on the disbursement of grants to, and maintenance of, public institutions in higher education. The entry regulatory functions of the AICTE, the MOI and the BCI would be performed by the IRAHE, so that their role would be limited to that of professional associations.

3. *Increase Public Spending and Diversify Sources of Financing*: The expansion of our system of higher education is not possible without enhanced levels of financing. This must necessarily come from both public and private sources.

- Since government financing will remain the cornerstone, government support for higher education should increase to at least 1.5 per cent of GDP, out of a total of at least 6 per cent of GDP for education.
- Even this would not suffice for the massive expansion in higher education that is an imperative. It is essential to explore other possibilities that can complement the increase in public expenditure.
- Most public universities are sitting on a large reservoir of untapped resources in the form of land. It should be possible to draw up norms and parameters for universities to use their available land as a source of finance.
- It is for universities to decide the level of fees but, as a norm, fees should meet at least 20 per cent of the total expenditure in universities. This should be subject to two conditions: first, needy students should be provided with a fee waiver plus scholarships to meet their costs; second, universities should not be penalised by the UGC for the resources raised from higher fees through matching deductions from their grants-in-aid.
- We should nurture the tradition of philanthropic contributions through changes in incentives for universities and for donors. At present, there is an implicit disincentive in both tax laws and trust laws. These laws should be changed so that universities can invest in financial instruments of their choice and use the income from their endowments to build up a corpus.
- Universities should also seek to tap other sources such as alumni contributions and licensing fees. We need to create supportive institutional mechanisms that allow universities to engage professional firms for this purpose.

- It is essential to stimulate private investment in education as a means of extending educational opportunities. It may be possible to leverage public resources, especially in the form of land grants, to attract more (not-for-profit) private investment.

4. *Establish 50 National Universities*: We recommend the creation of 50 National Universities that can provide education of the highest standard. As exemplars for the rest of the nation, these universities shall train students in a variety of disciplines, including humanities, social sciences, basic sciences, commerce and professional subjects, at both the undergraduate and post-graduate levels. The number 50 is a long term objective. In the short run, it is important to begin with at least 10 such universities in the next 3 years. National Universities can be established in two ways, by the government, or by a private sponsoring body that sets up a Society, Charitable Trust or Section 25 Company.

Since public finance is an integral constituent of universities worldwide, most of the new universities shall need significant initial financial support from the government. Each university may be endowed with a substantial allocation of public land, in excess of its spatial requirements. The excess land can be a subsequent source of income generation. Exceptions need to be made in existing income tax laws to encourage large endowments. Further, there should be no restriction on the utilisation of income in any given period or in the use of appropriate financial instruments. And these universities should have the autonomy to set student fee levels and tap other sources for generating funds.

The National Universities we propose shall admit students on an all-India basis. They shall adopt the principle of *needs-blind admissions*. This will require an extensive system of scholarships for needy students. Undergraduate degrees in the National Universities, in a three-year programme, should be granted on the basis of completing a requisite number of credits, obtained from different courses. The academic year shall therefore be semester-based and students shall be internally evaluated at the end of each course. Transfer of credits from one National University to another shall also be possible. An appropriate system of appointments and incentives is required to maximise the productivity of faculty in these National Universities. Strong linkages shall be forged between teaching and research, universities and industry, and universities and research laboratories. The National Universities shall be department-based and shall not have any affiliated colleges.

B. Excellence

5. *Reform Existing Universities*: Our endeavour to transform higher education must reform existing institutions. Some steps are listed below:

- Universities should be required to revise or restructure curricula at least once in three years.
- Annual examinations, which test memory rather than understanding, should be supplemented with continuous internal assessment which could begin with a weight of 25 per cent in the total to be raised to 50 per cent over a stipulated period.
- We propose a transition to a course credit system where degrees are granted on the basis of completing a requisite number of credits from different courses, which provides students with choices.
- Universities must become the hub of research once again to capture synergies between teaching and research that enrich each other. This requires not only policy measures but also changes in resource allocation, reward systems and mindsets.
- There must be a conscious effort to attract and retain talented faculty members through better working conditions combined with incentives for performance.
- The criteria for resource allocation to universities should seek to strike a much better balance between providing for salaries or pensions and providing for maintenance, development or investment. It should also recognise the

importance of a critical minimum to ensure standards and strategic preferences to promote excellence.

- The elements of infrastructure that support the teaching-learning process, such as libraries, laboratories and connectivity, need to be monitored and upgraded on a regular basis.
- There is an acute need for reform in the structures of governance of universities that do not preserve autonomy and do not promote accountability. Much needs to be done, but two important points deserve mention. The appointments of Vice-Chancellors must be freed from direct or indirect interventions on the part of governments, for these should be based on search processes and peer judgment alone. The size and composition of University Courts, Academic Councils and Executive Councils, which slow down decision-making processes and sometimes constitute an impediment to change, need to be reconsidered on a priority basis.
- We need, and should strive to create, smaller universities which are responsive to change and easier to manage.

6. *Restructure Undergraduate Colleges*: The system of affiliated colleges for undergraduate education, which may have been appropriate 50 years ago, is no longer adequate or appropriate and needs to be reformed. Indeed, there is an urgent need to restructure the system of undergraduate colleges affiliated to universities.

- The most obvious solution is to provide autonomy to colleges either as individual colleges or as clusters of colleges, on the basis of criteria. However, this would be able to provide a solution for a limited proportion, or number, of undergraduate colleges.
- Some of these affiliated colleges could be remodelled as community colleges, which could provide both vocational education and formal education.

- A Central Board of Undergraduate Education should be established, along with State Boards of Undergraduate Education, which would set curricula and conduct examinations for undergraduate colleges that choose to be affiliated with them. These Boards would separate the academic functions from the administrative functions and, at the same time, provide quality benchmarks.
- New undergraduate colleges could be established as community colleges, could be affiliated with the Central Board of Undergraduate Education or State Boards of Undergraduate Education, or could be affiliated with some of the new universities that are established.

7. *Promote Enhanced Quality*: The higher education system must provide for accountability to society and create accountability within. An expansion of higher education which provides students with choices and creates competition between institutions is going to be vital in enhancing accountability.

- There should be stringent information disclosure norms for all educational institutions, such as, their financial situation, physical assets, admissions criteria, faculty positions, academic curricula, as also their source and level of accreditation.
- Evaluation of courses and teachers by students as well as peer evaluation of teachers by teachers should be encouraged.
- There must be a focus on upgrading infrastructure, improving the training of teachers and continuous assessment of syllabi and examination systems.
- It is particularly important to enhance the ICT infrastructure. Websites and web-based services would improve transparency and accountability. A portal on higher education and research would increase interaction and accessibility. A knowledge network would connect all universities and colleges for online open resources.

- It may be necessary to rethink the issue of salary differentials within and between universities along with other means of attracting and retaining talented faculty members. Such salary differentials between and within universities could be effective without being large.
- It is necessary to formulate appropriate policies for the entry of foreign institutions into India and the promotion of Indian institutions abroad, while ensuring a level playing field for foreign and domestic institutions within the country.
- The system of higher education must recognise that there is bound to be diversity and pluralism in any system of higher education, and avoid a uniform one-size-fits-all approach. This sense of pluralism must recognise, rather than ignore or shy away from, such diversity and differentiation.

C. Inclusion

8. *Ensure Access for All Deserving Students*: Education is the fundamental mechanism for social inclusion through the creation of more opportunities. It is, therefore, essential to ensure that no student is denied the opportunity to participate in higher education due to financial constraints. We propose the following measures:

- Institutions of higher education should be encouraged to adopt a needs blind admissions policy. This would make it unlawful for educational institutions to take into account any financial factor while deciding whether or not to admit a student.
- There must be a well-funded and extensive National Scholarship Scheme targeting economically underprivileged students and students from historically socially disadvantaged groups.

9. *Affirmative Action*: A major aim of the higher education system must be to ensure that access to education for

economically and historically socially underprivileged students is enhanced in a substantially more effective manner.

- Reservations are essential but they are only a part, and one form, of affirmative action.
- Disparities in educational attainments are related to caste and social groups, but are also strongly related to other indicators such as income, gender, region and place of residence. Therefore, we need to develop a meaningful and comprehensive framework that would account for the multi-dimensionality of differences that still persist. For example, a deprivation index could be used to provide weighted scores to students and the cumulative score could be used to supplement a student's school examination score.

The recommendations set out in our letter require action at three different levels: reforms within existing systems, changes in policies, and amendments in, or the introduction of, new statutes or legislation. The suggested changes would also be implemented at three different levels: universities, state governments and the central government. As a next step, we would like to meet with you and concerned colleagues to work out the modalities of implementation.

In conclusion, it is important for us to recognise that there is a quiet crisis in higher education in India which runs deep. And the time has come to address this crisis in a systematic, forthright manner. Our recommendations in this letter constitute an important beginning. The changes suggested by us are essential and would make a real difference. Of course, the process of reform and change is continuous. And there is more to be done. We are writing to you, separately, about vocational education. We do recognise that a comprehensive reform of the school system is necessary to ensure that every child has an equal opportunity to enter the world of higher education.

We are convinced that it is important to act here and now. At the same time, we believe that there is an opportunity in this crisis. Given the demographic reality of a young India, expansion, inclusion and excellence in higher education can drive economic development and social progress. Indeed, what we do in the sphere of higher education now can transform economy and society in India by 2025.

VOCATIONAL EDUCATION

Observations

The National Knowledge Commission (NKC) considers Vocational Education and Training (VET) as an important element of the nation's education initiative. In order for VET to play its part effectively in the changing national context and for India to enjoy the fruits of the demographic dividend, there is an urgent need to redefine the critical elements of imparting vocational education to make them flexible, contemporary, relevant, inclusive and creative. The Government is well aware of the important role of VET and has already taken a number of important initiatives.

Recommendations

Through consultations with industry groups, academics, civil society and practitioners, NKC has deliberated ways and means to strengthen these initiatives and recommends the following long and short term strategies:

1. *Place Vocational Education Entirely Under the Ministry of Human Resource Development (MHRD)*: In view of the role of VET in human resource development and importance of its linkages with other streams of education, placing all aspects of VET under MHRD may be considered by the Government. Currently, VET falls under the purview of MHRD as well as the Ministry of Labour, which leads to fragmented management of the VET framework. MHRD may consider setting up a National Institute of Vocational Education Planning and Development to formulate strategy, advise the Government, and undertake research and development in areas pertaining to technology and workforce development.

2. *Increase the flexibility of VET within the mainstream education system* through the following steps:

(i) Aspects of general education (such as, numeracy skills, etc.) should be retained in VET as far as possible, to enable students to return to mainstream education at a later stage.

(ii) Courses in training institutes and polytechnics should have distinct tracks for students of different educational attainments.

(iii) Entry requirements for certain trades should reflect the requirement of the trade (as appropriate, for instance the entry requirement of Class X could be relaxed to Class VIII in some cases). Students should be permitted multiple entry and exit options in the vocational education stream.

(iv) Links should be established between the vocational education stream and school education as well as higher education.

(v) Courses devoted to certain skills training at the primary and secondary level should be introduced in all schools.

(vi) Vocational training should be made available in various literacy and adult education schemes.

(vii) Schemes for lifelong skill upgradation, through short training programmes, should be introduced.

(viii) There should be a provision for generating a cadre of multi-skilled persons.

3. *Quantify and Monitor the Impact of Vocational Education*: Data should be collected periodically and analysed in order to assess the impact of training on employability. Empirical evidence on wage premium or other advantages enjoyed by VET graduates; seat utilisation in training institutes; nature of employment post-training; efficacy of various schemes, etc. is essential for continuous improvement. A detailed exercise of manpower analysis is a necessary step to understand the nature and quantum of demand for VET and the mismatch between the skills of VET certificate holders and the requirements of

the labour market. This exercise may be undertaken by the proposed National Institute of Vocational Education Planning.

4. *Increase Resource Allocation to Vocational Education*: In per capita terms vocational education is costlier than general education, however, public expenditure on vocational education has been extremely low, as compared to general secondary education. Given the demand for skilled manpower in manufacturing and services the Government should aim to spend at least 10-15% of its total public expenditure on education, on vocational education.

Some options that may be considered for raising additional funds to finance a modernised VET scheme are:

(i) Enhancing fees, coupled with student loan schemes. This would also make VET institutions more responsive to market needs.
(ii) Raising funds through a cess on employers (for instance 2% of salaries of all employees, as in Singapore).
(iii) Making it obligatory for companies to finance public vocational education and training programmes (as in Korea).

5. *Expand Capacity Through Innovative Delivery Models*: In order to meet the burgeoning requirements of skilled and unskilled labour, a massive increase in quantity of training is needed. The Government may explore new delivery models to increase capacity such as public private partnerships, decentralised delivery, distance learning and computerised vocational training. At the same time, the Government must introduce certain minimum standards as a measure of quality and ensure that these are adhered to by all public and private VET institutions.

6. *Enhance the Training Options Available for the Unorganised and Informal Sector*: The greatest challenge lies in providing training for potential entrants in the unorganised/informal sector, which accounts for the largest proportion of employment. Systematic efforts need to be made to impart the skills required by the unorganised sector. These should be

formally introduced in the curricula and practical training courses. This aspect of VET is critical for the success of the system as a whole.

7. *Strengthen the Current Institutional Structure*: The existing Industrial Training Institutes (ITIs) and Industrial Training Centres (ITCs) are widely recognised to face problems, such as, poor quality trainers, lack of flexibility, outdated infrastructure, etc. Measures to improve the existing institutions are as follows:

(i) Extent of functional autonomy must be increased. ITIs should be given more power to strengthen and adapt their training programmes to better meet local market needs.
(ii) Indicators of internal and external efficiency should be developed (by the proposed National Institute) to incentivise good performance.
(iii) Modules on literacy, numeracy, communication skills, entrepreneurship and other general skills relevant to workplace requirements must be introduced in all courses.
(iv) Different tracks within courses for different levels of specialisation should be introduced.
(v) Students should be offered incentives such as tools, membership of trade associations, etc. as part of their degree/diploma.
(vi) Industry and trade involvement should be enhanced not only at the internship stage, but also at the time of examinations and placements.
(vii) Curricula should be constantly monitored and updated.
(viii) The skills and courses offered should be reviewed periodically. The number of skills currently offered needs to be increased.
(ix) Teaching should be conducted in English as well as local languages.
(x) Infrastructure should be regularly upgraded.
(xi) Quality of teaching should be drastically improved.

8. *Ensure a Robust Regulatory and Accreditation Framework*: In order to achieve the desired modernisation and expansion outlined above, a critical aspect will be regulating entry of new institutions and accreditation of all institutions. It is therefore recommended that an independent regulatory agency for VET be established. This body would license accreditation agencies and prescribe standards for certification. The procedures and methodologies adopted by the body would need to be simple and transparent to ensure unhindered growth in the sector.

9. *Ensure Proper Certification*: At present the process of certification is handled by the National Council for Vocational Training (NCVT), in association with State Councils for Vocational Training (SCVTs). Clear demarcation between the roles of the NCVT, the SCVTs and the DGE&T is essential for the proper functioning of the certification process. In order to ensure recognition of certification by employers, both in India and abroad, an electronic database of certified training providers as well as electronic identification for certified workers should be introduced. Electronic identification should contain information regarding skills and qualifications (and eventually other relevant information as well) about certified individuals and can be used in order to facilitate mobility of workers, encourage bank linkages and entrepreneurial initiatives etc.

10. *Undertake a Re-branding Exercise*: It is widely recognised that a crucial problem with vocational training in India is a negative association with manual labour. In order to match the modern requirement of the skills and competitiveness of the workforce a massive re-branding exercise is of the highest priority. This could be the prime task of the recently announced National Skills Mission. Initiatives, such as, replacing the use of terms such as 'vocational education' by 'skill development' are a step in the right direction. Efforts should be made by training institutes to chart out a career path for their students and introduce entrepreneurship training modules.

In conclusion, it is essential to significantly increase public and private investment in VET. However, a detailed analysis of manpower requirements in terms of numbers, skills and competitiveness is essential before formulating a master plan and deciding the quantum of expenditure in the 11th Plan. A robust framework needs to be put in place as a visible and dedicated resource in the MHRD is a pre-requisite in order to ensure quality and facilitate significant private investment and participation. Most importantly, the quality as well as the image of VET needs to be actively promoted in order for it to be viewed as comparable, and as relevant as general secondary education. (*Source:* National Knowledge Commission Website)

VIEWS EXPRESSED BY EMINENT EDUCATIONISTS ON THE NATIONAL KNOWLEDGE COMMISSION REPORT ON HIGHER EDUCATION

Various eminent educationists have expressed their views in the format, observe articles and comments on the National Knowledge Commission. These were published in the special issue of 'University News' Vol. 45.

Extracts of their views are as follows:

- There may be differing perceptions on different issues and dimensions of higher education. But it should be acknowledged that the NKC has given a newer paradigm of thinking and action, worth perusing with an open and positive mindset. As has always been the case, the power centers, including those at the helm of different regulatory bodies would use all the power/ lobby at their command to cleverly scuttle the recommendations of NKC. The Prime Minister Dr. Manmohan Singh who appointed the NKC would do well steer clear of all the power game and ensure the implementation of NKC's report in the real spirit.

  C. Thangamuthu,
  Former Vice Chancellor,
  Bharti Dosen University, Tiruchirapalli

- The Knowledge Commission has done well in reviewing the education system as a third umpire. Such a third party assessment (beyond the providers and institutions) is essential for national development. Internal reports—annual or occasional-will never bring out the weaknesses of an institution, agency or a system. Inherently they tend to be rosy highlighting only of the minor successes but not the failures. NKC has also underlined that there is a knowledge domain existing beyond the formal education. NKC had recommended some drastic measures to prepare the system of education to meet the demands of the new century. They cannot be postponed, if the nation has to compete with the other nations of the world and sustain its current growth rate. Such a periodic third party analysis and mid-term corrections are important for the planned development of any sector and more so for this key sector.

A. Gnanam,
Former President, Association of
Indian Universities and Former Chairman N.A.A.C.

- The NKC has made a series of useful and important suggestions on funding, governance of universities, promotion of quality, cluster of colleges, accountability, accreditation, access, affirmative action, faculty, incentives, for good performance, standardization of fees and fellowships for students. These are mostly repetitions of recommendations in earlier reports, with some difference in emphasis. It has been stated that:

  "A Nation or a society must carry out periodically mini revolutions, if that does not happen it must be prepared for major revolution."

  We have failed to carry out mini revolutions periodically and allowed certain interested associations and organizations to resist successfully all attempts at reform. It is necessary now to bring about a major revolution.

  It is my considered opinion that the Report on Higher Education of NKC, in so far as it is acceptable, may be implemented with a time frame and on a Mission Mode to bring about the much needed major revolution.

Dr. V.C. Kulandai Swamy

- The Ministry of Human Resource Development may initiate some policy measures in the wake of technological advancements and general socio-economic changes.
  - Central government/U.G.C/ State government must draw up enabling policies signifying the importance of financial support to meet the 'capacity' related needs, emerging and growing costs especially in terms of infrastructure, ICT and outstanding faculty to achieve the noble objectives of higher education. Otherwise innovative curriculum and infrastructure facilities will have no relevance.
  - State Universities have to be funded adequately for not only improving the quality but also sustain the quality.
  - Higher education institutions, need to be autonomous for effective functioning. They need to have wider exposure in establishing academic linkages with national and international Universities and organizations for enhancing the quality of the curricular offerings, teaching learning and research.
  - Policy framework for addressing all issues related to privatization and internationalization should be developed. Guidelines have to be developed for all types of collaborations to ensure continuity of operations, maintaining quality in all joint operations including research and patent development.
  - National Knowledge Commission Report's recommendations require action towards policy formulation, which will enable appropriate systemic actions by the institutions. These changes may synergize the roles at all levels of education system involving all the stakeholders.

Mariamma A. Varghese,
Former Vice Chancellor, SNDT University, Mumbai,
Senior Educational Consultant NAAC

Basically, the Knowledge Commission does not recognise the importance of public education and the significant role that the state plays in the development of higher education for it to contribute to national development in most civilised parts of the world. What is pity!

Jandhyala B.G. Tilak
Professor and Head Deptt. of Educational Finance, National University of Educational Planning and Administration, New Delhi.

THE VITAL GAPS AND NEEDED INTERVENTIONS

Nalin K. Shastree
Professor Magadh University, Bodhgaya

The most important gap lies in the fact that the NKC has not taken into the consideration the human component of education and has totally ignored to evolve a creative mind, imbibed with values. If the overall task before the National Knowledge Commission is to take steps that will give India the 'knowledge edge' in the coming decades, i.e. to ensure that our country becomes a leader in the creation, application and dissemination of knowledge, how can the same be accomplished without evolving a credible mind? The Indian tradition of knowledge has moved around the concept of building character through education, which has also been adopted by the Indian Parliament through the New Education Policy and also by the Programme of Action (POA). Would a computer assisted doctor or engineer without caring for values be able to contribute for strengthening the Nation? The Nation requires brilliant teachers, because education systems become quality systems by subject competent and ethically strong teachers. Therefore, the NKC should have seen the process of recruitment of teachers in the universities.

If education is a preparation of self-awareness, it essentially indicates the fact that it must imbibe the learner to discover his right mind. The search for what is true, good and beautiful through discovery of the right mind is the exercise of his creative imagination and critical sensibilities. Deeply moved with the drudgeries in education, Gandhi emphasized on the dynamic aspect of education that presupposes the fact that true education opens wider avenues of discovery of the right mind. Therefore, Gandhi came up with his innovative idea of *Nai Talim;* his innovative education system through which the discovery of one's all-embracing personality could be successfully operated upon. Gandhi meant by his education as a harmonious blending of life and orientation to work in the unique personality of a learner, whose creative faculties of imagination will open out vistas of wider activities to be performed forth and, at the same time, will enable him to evaluate and/or appropriate the multitudinous dimensions of human tastes and temperaments in order to derive endless aesthetic pleasure. The body and mind of an individual learner are, therefore, inseparable entities, each contributing to the manifestations of a balanced personality. Gandhi used a poetic expression and he said that his education is not only thinking brain but thinking fingers.

The NKC has not realized that all the mechanical glory cannot be bereft of human potentiality enriched in creative awareness and critical acumen, which is the first ever identification of an educated person. The fact is needed to be emphasized that all culture and civilization arose from the confluence of the brain and the finger of man, which lead to awakening of creative consciousness and critical appreciation. Therefore, it should be hoped that a better synthesis of values with technologies would be ensured by the NKC for discovering the right mind, which is the soul of Indian tradition. They mean a lot to the system.

But the Question Remains—Can these Recommendations be Implemented? If so

(a) How to implement them? Any action plan?
(b) Who should take the initiative? And finally,
(c) Can there be a deadline for implementation of these recommendations and so on.

It may be a worth while exercise at this point, for NKC to devote sometime on making recommendations with regard to the above mentioned four aspects to make atleast this time they are implemented. It is assumed that the committee members have good grasp of field situation and proper understanding of powers vested with Central Govt., State Govt. and university authorities and the employment scenario in the universities and colleges (permanent, temporary, contract and per hour basis teachers) who are part of the system for several years by now, and the obligations on the university thereby, and if not obliged to them the court interventions and so on.

India being a diverse country and having one of the largest democracies of the world, with its own history and its back log, implementation has become the most difficult task at all levels for both central and state administration and even for university administration, whatever may be the policy or programme, ultimately it is the implementation that matters. To implement these we need quality people, and, of course, they are in plenty, (proved by Indians all over the world) Yet it doesn't get implemented. Why? An action research on this may be worth while exercise.

It is time to get into research on some of the recommendations made again and again, but not yet implemented on the ground in spite of all good intentions of all those concerned.

No doubt, there are few new recommendations which we may hope for implementation soon. For example e-governance (not Data entry), Language Policy, Library Network, Networking of Institutions, Increase in Public spending, private participation etc. Let us hope that this time we see it on the ground instead of black and white in shelfs.

K. Sudha Rao
Professor & Head Department of Educational Policy,
NUEPA

REPORT OF THE NATIONAL LEVEL DISCUSSION ON THE REPORT OF THE NATIONAL KNOWLEDGE COMMISSION

A two-day National Level Discussion Meeting of eminent experts was organised by the National University of

Educational Planning and Administration, New Delhi on September 3-4, 2007 to critically review the recommendations of the National Knowledge Commission that submitted its report, *Report to the Nation 2006* to the Prime Minister a few months ago. Several distinguished experts and officials from Central and State governments have participated in it.

Among those who attended include P.M. Bhargava, former Vice Chairman of the Commission, Tapas Majumdar, M. Anandkrishnan, Amrik Singh, Amresh Bagchi, J. Veera Raghavan, A.K. Sharma, H.P. Dikshit, K.N. Chandrasekharan Pillai, Atul Sharma, D.N. Rao, Vinod Raina, Brahm Prakash, Kiran Datar, Madhu Prasad, Vijender Sharma, Arjun Dev, Chandana Chakarvarty, V.K. Tiwari, apart from the faculty from NUEPA including its Vice Chancellor Ved Prakash, Jandhyala B.G. Tilak, R. Govinda, K. Sudha Rao and Sudhanshu Bhushan. But for a brief presence of Jayati Ghosh that too for a very short period, none of the members of the National Knowledge Commission attended the meeting.

The participants discussed both the process of making the recommendations and the Report, and the recommendations along with their implications. There were remarks that the process of making the Report and submission of recommendations to the Prime Minister was not transparent enough. It did not involve public discussions and consultations with educationists the way it should have been, nor did it have even structured and formal discussions within the Commission. Since the recommendations were not even discussed within the Commission, one cannot say that there was any consensus or any compromise on the Report. Even the reports of the working groups of the Commission were not adequately considered in making the report, it was observed. Nevertheless, it was felt that since the Report was submitted to the Prime Minister, and it has some important recommendations with varied implications, it is necessary to discuss the Report.

According to a member of the Commission, NKC should not be viewed as any other normal commission or committee and the Report should not be seen as a report. The methodology adopted by the Commission was to send a series of letters to the Prime Minister as and when the Commission feels, on several issues that come under the terms of reference of the Commission, and not to make any report *per se*. Hence it should be seen as a set of communications from the Commission to the Prime Minister. If this is so, there is a danger: while one can expect a coherent set of well-reasoned proposals in a report, a series of letters or commutations may end up with making a few random proposals and piece-meal solutions, not necessarily knit together. Such an approach also does not allow the Commission to have a comprehensive and holistic approach to the education sector. It is also not clear whether these letters will be in public domain at least after they are submitted to the Prime Minister, if not before, so that meaningful public discussions would take place.

The Commission made several recommendations in the 'Report'—some new, some not so new, many controversial and perhaps very few relevant.

The three general comments made by the expert participants of the meeting on the Report are as follows:

- First, the a historical approach adopted by the NKC on many issues was indeed appalling. The Commission did not note strengths and weaknesses of the system as it developed over several decades, if not centuries. Nor did it take into account the current status of the system, the recommendations made by several committees in the recent past some of which were acted upon and many not, the federal structure and the centre-state relations in education, the dangerous implications of reduced role of the government and increased role of the private sector in education, internationalisation of education merely for economic gains, etc.
- Second, the NKC seems to have taken a fragmented outlook of the education sector, rather than looking at it in a holistic way. It makes some proposals on some sub-sectors of education — elementary education (only on right to education), vocational education and training and some on higher education, apart from brief

comments on libraries, languages, translation, knowledge network, e-governance, etc. The predominant focus of the report is on education; but it is not a report on education, nor is it of course a commission on education.

- Third, neither the rationale for the recommendations, nor the implications and the details on implementation of the proposals made are described in the Report.

Besides the very nature of the report, participants of the meeting discussed in detail many of the recommendations made by the NKC on education.

While the NKC favoured a Central legislation on the right to education, it was observed that the NKC did not grasp the whole issue, as originally articulated in the famous Unnikrishnan judgment of the Supreme Court in 1993 that highlighted the links between the right to live and the right to education, as enshrined in the Constitution of India. Nor did it go into details on the recent controversies raised during the CABE and subsequent meetings on making the Right to Education Bill. Of course the NKC promised to make a broader set of recommendations on school education in near future. But no such recommendations seem to have been made during the last several months after the report was published in January 2007. As a member of the NKC reported, much work is in progress and more letters are in the pipeline to be sent to the Prime Minister on educational issues, including specifically on school education. It appears that the NKC has expressed doubts on the data used by the Planning Commission on enrolments, teachers and students that include non-formal education systems, including EGS schools, bridge course centres and Para teachers. It is also concerned about the rigidity of the SSA norms, teacher training facilities and lack of infrastructure, and the syllabi and examination system.

The view that the country will go broke if it were to spend the required resources on making elementary education a fundamental right, was resented by many participants in the meeting. The classic Confucius dictum, also made by Alfred

Marshall, is: 'no nation goes bankrupt by investing in education of its people.'

The major omissions in the Report, according to the participants, inter alia, relate to teacher education and teacher training. Teacher education is in a dismal state, while the shortages of teachers are increasingly felt at almost at all levels of education.

Several recommendations relating to higher education were found to be quite controversial. They include setting up of the Independent Regulating Authority for Higher Education (IRAHE), restructuring and reduced scope of functions of the UGC, dismantling of some national level bodies, setting up of central boards of undergraduate education, etc. Some found the setting up of the IRAHE and central board of undergraduate education desirable proposals, but many were skeptical on the efficiency of these proposed new structures that are expected to replace some of the existing structures; some also felt that it would affect the federal structure. The Commission, some members felt, did not have a fair understanding of the history, structure and functions and the functioning of some of the existing institutions. They, however, admit that there is a plenty of scope for reforming the existing institutions.

While the Commission recommended raising of student fees to at least 20 per cent of the recurring expenditure on higher education institutions, some felt that it could be the maximum and not the minimum, as any raise beyond this level will be affecting socio-economic equity dimensions in education. Some questioned even the rationale for the numbers—number of universities recommended, and the rationale for the elitist proposal of setting up 50 national universities.

There are some who appreciated and many questioned the recommendations of the Commission on privatisation, and on trade in education, though these recommendations or even the arguments made by the participants are not altogether new. Privatisation and internationalisation of (trade in) education mutually feed on each other.

In the increasingly globalised contemporary world, many view that internationalisation of higher education is an unalterable component. Even many educationists do find virtues in internationalisation of higher education; after all, universities are and should be universal in their nature and scope. Also, this has been there for several centuries. However, the new dimension of trade in education is a matter of contention in internationalisation. Few question the old mode, but many have serious reservations on the emerging modes of internationalisation. It was observed that before one thinks of internationalisation of our higher education system, it is necessary that our higher education system is raised to a level equivalent to the best systems in the world, so that competition becomes meaningful and will be between equals and not between unequals. So any move towards internationalisation will be counterproductive, if our system is not made an excellent one in terms of quality of education, quality of teachers and quality of graduates it produces. It might require huge public investments in education. But that is necessary. We have left our system severely-under invested all these years.

If there is one coherent and consistent line of thinking that underlines the whole Report that is relating to private sector in education. The NKC strongly favoured an increased role of the private sector in education under different forms—public-private partnerships, diversification of financing of higher education, stimulating private investments and setting up of private institutions. Some welcomed the role of the private sector in education as (a) the state does not have much money and (b) it may improve competition and quality. It was also felt that philanthropic private sector needs to be encouraged. Many participants highlighted the limits of privatisation and the danger of privatisation leading to commercialisation of education. Perhaps Indian higher education is more privatised than most other systems of higher education in developing and developed countries with very few exceptions, in terms of number of private institutions and enrolments in private institutions; and it is already highly commercialised, posing problems relating to access and equity. It is also crowding out the public institutions. Some of those who argue in favour of private sector also stressed the need to recognise that private sector will necessarily go for profits, and they also need to be regulated. But unfortunately in practice the difference between (non-philanthropic) privatisation and commercialisation is very thin. Privatisation is viewed as a solution to the public inadequacies; but an improved public system may be the best solution to the problems created by the private system. Perhaps this will also be a measure that checks the trends in internationalisation. Improvement in the public education system is of course very important on its own.

The participants of the meeting stressed the need to critically examine each recommendation in great detail and to look at alternatives available before it is implemented. Many participants felt that most recommendations are elitist in nature and doubted whether such proposals would help in 'better and faster inclusive growth' — the goal of the eleventh five year plan! The two-day discussion meeting coincided with media reports that the Planning Commission has accepted 'many' recommendations of the NKC. *Report by Prof. J.B.G. Tilak*

Source: University News, 45(48) November 26-December 02, 2007

Comment on the KCR by Anand Sarup (A Former Secretary Govt. Department of Education, MHRD, Government of India)

We don't have to Reinvent the Wheel to Learn What is What

This is not a commentary on the Report of the Knowledge Commission. Jandyala B.G. Tilak has already made some comments to show that the Knowledge Commission has dealt with one of the most crucial national issues in a cavalier fashion. It has made a "few highly general, pedestrian observations on the quality of higher education or on the governance of universities" without any in depth analysis and it has also not provided supporting evidence for its conclusions.

I apprehend that the report will meet the usual fate of such documents by being lauded at first and then being consigned to the cold storage. It is surprising that there has been almost no formal or informal consultation with either the state governments or the representatives of state institutions. This means that the National Knowledge Commission is unaware of the decisive role states and state institutions play in respect of education.

Anybody with a modicum of wisdom knows that what has happened before is likely to happen again unless conscious safeguards are built to prevent recurrence of misadventures. The last major effort for restructuring education was made in 1986 through the formulation of the National Policy on Education. This is what happened to the National Policy on Education 1986 also.

Once it was approved, not only by both houses of the Parliament, but also, by the National Development Council, the government decided to go on with the business as usual.

The Process of Policy Formulation

The process of policy formulation was attended by great optimism. There was a general suspension of the disbelief which usually attends any initiative of the government but once the highly visible business of making a new policy and getting it approved was over, the Ministry of Human Resource Development decided to take it easy and this change of attitude resulted in the scuttling of the newly formulated policy.

The essential rationale of formulating a new policy was to prepare, along with it, a detailed, effective and implementable Programme of Action (POA). During this phase of action, Shri P.V. Narasimha Rao, the Minister for MHRD was openly critical of any move to prolong the policy making phase any further. He wanted this exercise, which to some seemed at the heart of the whole effort, to be finished by producing some document which would be so bulky and complicated that no body would have the patience to read it. Unfortunately, many of the bureaucrats too wanted to start with the power driven phase of implementation. It is curious that on the very day the new policy was presented to CABE, in a presentation at the NUEPA.

It was explained as to how the new phase could easily go from implementation to the scuttling of the new policy.

During the exercise of setting up Working Groups for evolving a POA, the Minister for MHRD was repeatedly advised that the Ministry should prepare a framework for them. It was repeatedly explained that without such a framework, it would be impossible to produce a balanced POA.

Asking Working Groups to produce POA for their respective areas, without an overall framework, would be tantamount to commissioning different sculptors to produce parts of a human body without giving them any idea of the final dimensions of the statue into which these would be fitted. In such a situation, it was always possible that the nose would turn out to be longer than the forearm!

When nothing else availed, a quiet attempt was made to analyse the policy, paragraph by paragraph, to pinpoint the critical issues arising from it, in the hope that if the Minister realised the importance of the points made out, he might agree to these being sent out to the Working Groups charged with the responsibility of preparing subject-wise reports. Alas, even though the Minister went through the 'Workbook' prepared for the purpose and even made comments on it in his own hand, he totally refused to allow its issuance to the Working Groups. It was so discouraging to find him stuck on short circuiting the key exercise of preparing a POA which, he believed, even if it was without a design, would look impressive and get accepted by the Parliament. The story of this 'Workbook' was described at some length in the book: P.V. Narasimha Rao-Years of Power (Har-Anand Publications, 1993), published during the lifetime and the Primeministership of Shri Narasimha Rao. An incident relating to the 'Workbook' as presented in the above mentioned book shows that Mr. Rao understood the complexities of implementing the new policy but, in spite of this because he was suffering from the fatigue of policy making exercises, he ignored it and, in the process scuttled a great chance of evolving a POA which might have given the country a chance of permeating the policy with the dynamism essential for becoming a change agent.

In the chapter on 'Shaping the Education Policy' (pages 153-154), I have described, as follows, the way he dealt with the 'workbook': "Mr Rao was aware of the great store laid by the Prime Minster on the New Education Policy and was, at all times, equal to the task. Despite poor health, and continuous strain of working under the pressure, he weighed every word and phrase he put down including those which could lose their urgency with the passage of time."

"In one of the meetings, Mr. Narasimha Rao caught me indulging in mental absenteeism. He knew and was indulgent of this trait of mine. In this particular instance, he caught me concentrating on a type script. He asked me to show it to him, which I had no choice but to comply. After glancing casually at a few pages, he put it among his papers and turned his attention to the matters under discussion."

"After the meeting, when I tried to retrieve the type script, he asked me what it was about, why I had never shown it to him and what I planned to do with it. I told him that it was a highly disaggregated clause by clause analysis of the National Education Policy, 1986, which had just been approved by both houses of the Parliament and based on which, we had" to prepare a Programme of Action. I had prepared an analysis only for myself to make sure that at least would realise the complexity and, in some cases, the impossibility of fulfilling the obligations arising from the policy."

"A few days later, when I went to see him about something else, he quietly handed the typed material back to me. Later, when I went through the notes he had made in his own hand, I was greatly impressed with by his incisive understanding, not only of the scope and limitations of educational processes and institutions, but also of the constraints within which central government has to function in respect of many issues vis-a-vis the states."

I hope, after reading this material, the readers to enter into these deliberations with humility, avoiding sitting on judgement on various matters only from the intellectuals' viewpoint. The real world of decision making and management of change in education is very much more complicated that the chiaroscuro we can see from the windows of our libraries.

There is a multiplicity of forces at work all the time and there are so many vested interests wanting to protect the status quo. These can be ignored only at great risk. My most recent experience with the Ministry of Human Resource Development as the Chairman of the Task Force for Improvement in the System of Education (the experiences in respect of which have been documented stage by stage), has shown that both the political executives as well as the educational bureaucracy are completely impervious to the needs for improvement of the system of education. One day perhaps, on some other occasion these experiences in the Task Force for Improvement in the System of Education would get studied but, in the meanwhile, let us understand that general and analytically well supported statements should be approached with great caution.

If this message of approaching educational problems with humility, caution and systematic interaction with all the stakeholders, particularly the state governments and their institutions, gets across to the readers. I would feel that my feeble voice has been heard and may be, this one, the knowledge commission will achieve better results than earlier initiatives in this direction.

7

Renovation and Rejuvenation of Higher Education: Prof. Yash Pal Committee Report (2009)

APPIONTMENT OF THE COMMITTEE TO ADVISE ON RENOVATION AND REJUVENATION OF HIGHER EDUCATION

The Government of India appointed a committee on 28 February, 2008 to review the role of statutory bodies like the University grants Commission (UGC) and All India Council for Technical Education (AICTE) in the context of changes in higher, professional and technical education in the country and demands of a new knowledge economy.

Subsequently the nomenclature of the committee was changed as Committee to *'Advise on Renovation and Rejuvenation of Higher Education.'* (14 Oct. 2008). The committee submitted its first report in August 2008 and its final report in July 2009. The Committee consisted of 20 members including the Chairman. The major recommendation of the committee are given of the listing of office memorandum etc.

No. 4-4/2008-U.I (A)
Government of India
Ministry of Human Resource Development
[Department of Higher Education]

New Delhi, dated the 28th February, 2008

Notification

Subject: Constitution of a UGC/AICTE Review Committee to review the functions of UGC/AICTE in the wake of changes in higher, professional and technical education in India and demands of a new knowledge economy.

There is a need to review the role of statutory bodies like the University Grants Commission (UGC) and the All India Council for Technical Education (AICTE) in the context of changes in higher, professional and technical education in the country and demands of a new knowledge economy. Accordingly, the Government constitutes a Review Committee with the following members;

(i) Prof. Yashpal, former Chairman, University Grants Commission. - Chairman

(ii) Prof. N.R. Madhava Menon, Member, Centre-State Relations and former Vice Chancellor, National Law School, Bangalore and Director, National Judicial Academy, Bhopal - Member

(iii) Prof. Pulin B. Nayak, Professor, Department of Economics, Delhi School of Economics, University of Delhi. - Member

(iv) Prof. L.M. Patnaik, Professor of Computer Science, IISc, Bangalore. - Member

(v) Prof. Kaushik Basu, Professor of Economics and Karl Marx, Professor of International Studies, Deptt. of Economics, Uris Hall,—Cornell University. - Member

(vi) Shri S.V. Giri, former Secretary, Department of Education, Govt. of India and former Vice Chancellor, Sri Satya Sai Institute of Higher Learning, Prasanthi Nilayam, Puttaparthi, Andhra Pradesh. - Member

(vii)	Prof. J.K. Chaddha, former Vice Chancellor, JNU and present Member, Economic Advisory Council to the PM, Vigyan Bhawan Annexe, New Delhi.		- Member
(viii)	Prof. (Ms.) Malini Bhattacharya, Member, National Commission for Women.		- Member
(ix)	Prof. Goverdhan Mehta, Chairman, NAAC and Former Director, IISc, Bangalore.		- Member
(x)	Prof. Sukhadeo Thorat, Chairman, University Grants Commission		- Member
(xi)	Chairman, All India Council for Technical Education.		- Member
(xii)	One Vice Chancellor of a State University	To be nominated by the Ministry of HRD	- Member
(xiii)	One Secretary to a State Govt. dealing with Higher/ Technical Education.		- Member
(xiv)	Dr. Ramdas M. Pai, President, Manipal University.		- Member
(xv)	Prof. Ananda Krishnan, Chairman, IIT, Kanpur.		- Member
(xvi)	Prof. M.S. Ananth, Director, IIT, Chennai.		- Member
(xvii)	Prof. Pankaj Chandra, Director, IIM, Bangalore.		- Member
(xviii)	Prof. Mushirul Hasan, Vice Chancellor, Jamia Millia Islamia.		- Member

(xix)	Secretary, Planning Commission	- Member
(xx)	Finance Secretary, Govt. of India.	- Member
(xxi)	Secretary, Department of Higher Education, Government of India.	- Member
(xxii)	Joint Secretary [Higher Education], Department of Higher Education, Govt. of India.	- Ex-officio Member - Secretary

TERMS OF REFERENCE OF THE COMMITTEE

2. The following were the terms of reference of the Committee:
   (a) To review the functioning of the UGC/AICTE and to critically assess the role of the UGC/AICTE and their preparedness to provide institutional leadership to the emerging demands of access, equity, relevance and quality of higher education/technical education and the university system.
   (b) To review the provisions of the University Grants Commission Act 1956 and the All India Council for Technical Education Act, 1987 and various suggestions for amendments to the said Acts by earlier Committees such as the Prof. Amrik Singh Committee.
   (c) The role of the UGC in coordinating standards of higher education vis-à-vis the functional role of other statutory bodies such as AICTE, MCI, DCI, NCI, NCTE, DEC, etc.
   (d) An assessment of the requirements of autonomy of the UGC vis-à-vis the Central Government and that of the university system vis-à-vis the UGC.
   (e) The role of the UGC/AICTE in determining and enforcing standards of higher education/technical education in State Universities and the possibility

of introducing a system of incentives and disincentives so that national standards of higher education/technical education are not compromised or diluted.

(f) Recommendations in regard to an effective and efficient mechanism for flow of resources from the UGC to the universities for their timely utilization including a mechanism of feedback thereto.

(g) The requirement of transparency and efficiency in the functioning of the UGC/AICTE.

(h) The role of the UGC vis-à-vis declaration of institutions to be deemed universities and recommendations for streamlining the process adopted by the UGC.

(i) Recommendations about the need to change the eligibility criteria for becoming eligible to receive grants under Section 12B of the UGC Act 1956.

(j) Any other issue arising out of or relating to the above terms of reference and, the functioning of the UGC/AICTE which the Government or the Committee on its own, may desire to look into.

OFFICE MEMORANDUM

Subject: Constitution of a UGC/AICTE Review Committee to review the functions of UGC/AICTE in the wake of changes in higher, professional and technical education in India and demands of a new knowledge economy—naming of the Committee as 'Committee to Advise on Renovation and Rejuvenation of Higher Education.'

A Review Committee was constituted under the Chairmanship of Prof. Yash Pal, former Chairman, University Grants Commission vide this Ministry's Notification of even number dated 28th February, 2008 to review the role of statutory bodies like the University Grants Commission and the All India

Council for Technical Education in the context of changes in higher, professional and technical education in the country and demands of a new knowledge economy. The composition and the terms of reference of the Committee were indicated in that Notification.

2. It has been decided with the approval of the Competent Authority to name the said Committee as "Committee to Advise on Renovation and Rejuvenation of Higher Education."
3. The composition and the terms of reference of the Committee remain unchanged.

(Sunil Kumar)
Joint Secretary to the Government of India

LIST OF MEMBERS OF "COMMITTEE TO ADVISE ON RENOVATION AND REJUVENATION OF HIGHER EDUCATION"

1. Prof. Yash Pal
   Chairman
   UGC/AICTE Review Committee
   11-B, Super Deluxe Flats
   Sector-15 A NOIDA-201 301
2. Prof. (Dr.) N.R. Madhava Menon
   Member Commission on Centre-State Relations
   Vigyan Bhawan Annexe
   New Delhi-11
3. Prof. Pulin B.Nayak
   Deptt. of Economics,
   Delhi School of Economics
   Delhi University
   Delhi-110 007
4. Prof. L.M. Patnaik
   Vice Chancellor
   Defence Institute of Advanced Technology
   Girinagar, Pune

5. Prof. Kaushik Basu
   C. Marks Professor of International Studies and
   Professor of Economics and
   Director Centre for Analytic Economics,
   Deptt. of Economics, Cornell Univ. Ithaca,
   New York-14853
6. Shri S.V. Giri
   A/2 West Prasanthi-1
   Prasanthi Neelayam
   Ananthapur Distt.(A.P)-515134
7. Prof. G.K. Chadha
   (Former V.C., JNU)
   Vigyan Bhawan Annexe, New Delhi
8. Dr.(Smt.) Malini Bhattacharya
   Member, National Commission for Women,
   4 Deen Dayal Upadhyaya Marg
   New Delhi-110 002
9. Prof. Goverdhan Mehta
   Chairman
   National Assessment and Accreditation Council
   P.O. Box 1075, Nagarbhavi Circle
   Bangalore-560 072
10. Prof. Sukhadeo Thorat
    Chairman
    University Grants Commission
    Bahadur Shah Zafar Marg
    New Delhi-110 002
11. Prof. R.A. Yadav
    Chairman
    All India Council For Technical Education
    Chandralok Building, 7th Floor, Janpath,
    New Delhi
12. Prof. Vijay Khole
    Vice Chancellor
    University of Mumbai
    M.G. Road, Fort, Mumbai-400 032
13. Shri K. Ganesan
    Secretary
    Higher Education

Govt. of Tamil Nadu
Fort St. George
Chennai-600 009

14. Dr. Ramdas M. Pai
Chancellor
Manipal University
Madhav Nagar, Manipal-576 104
Udupi District, Karnataka State
15. Prof. M. Ananda Krishnan
Former Vice-Chancellor
Anna University
8/15 V Main Road, Madan Apartments 2nd Floor,
Kasturibhai Nagar Adyar, Chennai-600020
16. Prof. M.S. Ananth
Director
IIT, Madras, Chennai-600 036
17. Prof. Pankaj Chandra
Director
I.I.M Bangalore Bannerghatta Road
Bangalore-560 076
18. Prof. Mushirul Hasan
Vice Chancellor
Jamia Millia Islamia,
New Delhi-67
19. Dr. Subas Chandra Pani, Secretary
Planning Commission
Yojana Bhawan
Sansad Marg, New Delhi-1
20. Smt. Sushma Nath
Secretary (Expenditure)
Department of Expenditure
North Block,
New Delhi-110 001
21. Shri R.P. Agarwal,
Education Secretary, Shastri Bhawan
New Delhi-110 001
22. Shri Sunil Kumar
Joint Secretary (Hr. Edn.)

Member Secretary (Committee to Advise on Renovation and Rejuvenation of Higher Education)
Ministry of Human Resource Development
Deptt. of Higher Education
Shastri Bhawan,
New Delhi-110 001

23. Dr. Krishna Kumar
Director
NCERT
Shri Aurobindo Marg
New Delhi-110 016
24. Dr. Kiran Karnik
Former President
NASSCOM
Q2A Haus Khas Enclave New Delhi-21

Consultant:

Dr. Apoorvanand
Deptt. of Hindi University of Delhi
Delhi-110 007.

OBSERVATIONS CONTAINED IN THE INTERIM REPORT 27/8/08

Basic Elements of a New Organisation of Our Higher Education

Recognition that a university should encompass all disciplines and their interfaces.

The curriculum framework should recognize outside world and go across boundaries of disciplines.

All higher education institutions should move in this direction.

Higher education institutions need to be accredited and supported.

For this we need I single higher education commission (HEC).

This should be set up by the prime minister with the advice of a large academic college to be chosen in an appropriate way.

The HEC should be self renewing.

The HEC will have under it appropriate autonomous councils for various areas.

As an Umbrella organization HEC should play a catalytic role for interaction between different subject areas and different departments, institutions, universities, both public and private.

HEC and all its councils would invite proposals from all universities and would distribute the available resources, preferably as block grants.

Inspections and monitoring would be reduced drastically. The accredited universities would be respected.

These accredited universities would be charged with the responsibility of setting up and developing components and colleges in their areas of operation.

For the state universities State Councils of Higher Education might provide the interface between HEC and the universities. These councils will also not indulge in continuous inspection and monitoring. The Universities would be left alone.?

Other Thoughts

All IIT's should become full-fledged universities. They have shown a great capability for functioning excellent undergraduate institutions—some call them as factories for largely servicing the outside world. Because of various reasons, including their prowess, they attract very clever students.

This class of students has a potential far greater than they reach by graduating through a largely undergraduate level of competence in some engineering disciplines. Exposed to a broad based university curriculum and atmosphere IIT's have the potential to become first rate universities. Let them be the blue prints of first rate Central universities. Just think of MIT on which at least one of them was patterned. It would be nice to have a few Nobel prizes in various sciences, economics and communication coming from such transformed IIT's.

All Central Universities must have undergraduate education. The best academics, scientists and engineers should teach undergraduate classes. Most of our students are fossilized during undergraduate years. Incidentally this would be another point in favour of IIT's becoming Central Universities. Not just basic sciences, and social sciences but also medical sciences can be creative if coupled with good engineering and science creativity.

Similarly agricultural universities would gain a lot through becoming full-fledged universities encompassing the Universe of knowledge.

Vocational Education

There is no question that a society cannot function without a widespread development of vocational education. The parameters and conception of this education has been changing. Much of the present day education in computer applications, electronics and management is also vocational education.

The fact that demand for such education has increased and many private colleges have come up does not change the fact that these institutions are providing vocational education. The quality of this education is generally rather poor.

There is an impression that many of the private institutions are not doing a very good job in this regard, in spite of the fact that they charge rather heavy fees.

Yash Pal

AGENDA FOR RENOVATION AND REJUVENATION OF HIGHER EDUCATION: FINAL REPORT

The Committee made the following recommendations:

1. Creation of an all-encompassing National Commission for Higher Education and Research (NCHER), a Constitutional body to replace the existing regulatory bodies including the UGC, AICTE, NCTE and DEC and to follow up the Constitutional amendment with an appropriate law for the Commission's functioning;
2. Universities to be made responsible regarding the academic content of all courses and programmes of study including professional courses. Professional bodies like the AICTE, NCTE, MCI, BCI, COA, INC, PCI etc. to be divested of their academic functions, which would be restored to the universities;

3. Curricular reform to be the topmost priority of the newly created NCHER which would create a curricular framework based on the principles of mobility within a full range of curricular areas and integration of skills with academic depth;
4. It should be mandatory for all universities to have a rich undergraduate programme and undergraduate students must get opportunities to interact with the best faculty. While appointing teachers to the universities their affiliation to a particular college should also be specified to emphasize the need for their exposure to undergraduate students;
5. Undergraduate programmes to be restructured to enable students to have opportunities to access all curricular areas with fair degree of mobility. It is highly recommended that normally, no single discipline or specialized university should be created;
6. The vocational education sector is at present outside the purview of universities and colleges. Alienation of this sector can be overcome by bringing it under the purview of universities and by providing necessary accreditation to the courses available in polytechnics, industrial training institutions, and so on. Additionally the barriers to entry into universities for students going through vocational training should be lowered to enable them to upgrade their knowledge base at any stage of their careers;
7. The NCHER should also galvanize research in the university system through the creation of a National Research Foundation;
8. New governing structures to be evolved to enable the universities to preserve their autonomy in a transparent and accountable manner;
9. Practice of according status of deemed university be stopped forthwith till the NCHER takes a considered view on it. It would be mandatory for all existing deemed universities to submit to the new accreditation

norms to be framed on the lines proposed in this report within a period of three years failing which the status of university should be withdrawn. However, unique educational initiatives which have over a period of time enriched higher education by their innovations to be given recognition and supported appropriately;

10. Modern higher education system requires extension facilities, sophisticated equipment and highly specialized knowledge and competent teachers. It would not be possible for every university to possess the best of these infrastructures. Hence, one of the primary tasks of the NCHER to create several inter-university centres (IUCs) in diverse fields to create the best of these possibilities and attract the participation of several institutions of higher learning to avail them. The model already successfully demonstrated by the IUCs of the UGC like the Inter University Centre for Astronomy and Astrophysics, Inter University Accelerator Centre and others, would be a valuable guidance in their structures, governance, operation and support.
11. Institutions of excellence like the IITs and IIMs to be encouraged to diversify and expand their scope to work as full-fledged universities, while keeping intact their unique features, which shall act as pace-setting and model governance systems for all universities;
12. One of the first tasks of the NCHER should be to identify the best 1,500 colleges across India to upgrade them as universities, and create clusters of other potentially good colleges to evolve as universities.
13. Universities to establish live relationship with the real world outside and develop capacities to respond to the challenges faced by rural and urban economies and culture;
14. All levels of teacher education to be brought under the purview of higher education;
15. A national testing scheme for admission to the universities on the pattern of the GRE to be evolved

which would be open to all the aspirants of University education, to be held more than once a year. Students would be permitted to send their best test score to the university of their choice.

16 Quantum of Central financial support to State-funded universities, be enhanced substantially on an incentive pattern, keeping in view the needs for their growth;

17. Expansion of the higher education system to be evaluated and assessed continuously to excel and to respond to the needs of different regions in India in order to ensure not only equity and access but also quality and opportunity of growth along the academic vertical. The NCHER too should be subject to external review once in five years.

18. Establish a National Education Tribunal with powers to adjudicate on disputes among stake-holders within institutions and between institutions so as to reduce litigation in Courts involving universities and higher education institutions; and

19. Set up a Task Force to follow up on the implementation of this Agenda for Action within a definite time-frame.

ROLE OF THE NATIONAL COMMISSION FOR HIGHER EDUCATION AND RESEARCH (NCHER)

- While acting as the apex regulatory body in the field of higher education in India it creates an enabling environment for universities to become self-regulatory bodies;
- Becomes the premier advisory body to the Central and State Governments on policy issues regarding higher education in India;
- Prepares and presents a Report on the State of Higher Education in India annually to Parliament;
- Serves as a think tank on higher education policy in the country: provides a vision of higher education to be reflected in a curriculum framework, benchmarks universities, compares with institutions globally,

develops requirements of disciplines, proposes new education policies both for Central and the State institutions, and evaluates the costs and price of education;

- The Commission would create appropriate norms, processes and structures for ensuring quality and accrediting universities;
- Establishes transparent norms and process for entry and exist of institutions—the need is to make the process easy for good and serious proposals for setting up new institutions;
- Develops sources and mechanisms of funding for universities and other institutions, including for research;
- Initiates measures to ensure that governance in universities is done in a transparent and accountable manner;
- Provides the mechanism for a national database on higher education;
- Helps in creating an environment in academic institutions that is conducive to bring young people to take up academia as a career;
- Creates soft processes for interaction between students and teachers;
- Lightens the load of Universities, by developing a scheme to gradually free the universities of the colleges affiliated to them.

STRUCTURE OF THE NATIONAL COMMISSION FOR HIGHER EDUCATION AND RESEARCH (NCHER)

The National Commission for Higher Education and Research (NCHER) has to be a body, which would inspire confidence in the academic community of India and serve as the voice of the academic community related to higher education and gains the serious attention of policy-makers. Its structure and composition and the process of its formation has to be such that it acquires an autonomous character of its own.

The NCHER would be an autonomous body created by making a suitable amendment to the Constitution, accountable only to the Indian parliament and drawing its budgetary resources from the Ministry of Finance. It would have a seven-member board with a full-time Chairperson. Of the seven members, one would be an eminent professional from the world of industry and one with the background of a long and consistent social engagement. All other five members would be academic people of eminence, representing broad areas of knowledge.

The structure of the National Commission for Higher Education and Research would not be top heavy and its role would be free of excessive centralization of regulation of universities and colleges. The status of the Chairperson of the commission should be analogous to that of the Chief Election Commissioner and that of the members should be comparable to the Election Commissioners.

The Process of identifying the Chairperson and members should be vested with a search committee comprising the Prime Minister, the Leader of the Opposition in Parliament and the Chief Justice of India in consultation with a Collegium consisting of eminent academics, learned academies and prestigious institutions relating to the fields of knowledge in diverse fields.

The Chairperson of the NCHER should be invited to appear before both the Houses of the Parliament or its Committees and appraise the members about the state of Higher Education in India and the directions for its growth and development. While the NCHER is expected to devise its own processes and structure for functioning, it is suggested that the Commission may initially consist of five divisions. These are suggested to be as follow:

Future Directions: Developing global benchmarks on student performance; university performance; salaries, potential programmers; new research directions; and articulation of needs of the government in terms of manpower etc.

Accreditation Management: Creating norms for accreditation and certifying multiple accreditation agencies which would be independent of the government. Institutions and universities may like to get accreditation from one or more than one agencies depending on their reputation. They would be also providing annual feedback to universities, and organizing workshops etc.

Funding and Development: Developing funding needs of universities, developing mechanisms for funding institutions, helping universities with development of corpus and good endowment management, managing the guaranteed student loan/scholarship programme, and funding the requirements of universities etc.

New Institutions and Incubation: Including training workshops for first-time VCs as well as on themes like accounting, investing the corpus, communication within and outside the university, negotiations and managing vendors, good office practices, human resource management etc.

Information and Governance: This division will focus on managing the data needs of the commission, display of information on universities, develop performance parameters on the governance of universities, support other divisions with information as well as provide students with information on each university. This division will also inform the Accreditation and Funding and Development divisions of the performance or lack thereof, for each university, each year.

An eminent academic with a tenure of five years would head each division. Each board member would be an overseer of one or two of the divisions. Each division will have an advisory board. The advisory board will comprise eminent persons from India or abroad.

The Chairperson and the five heads of the above-mentioned divisions would form the executive body of the commission, which would oversee all its functions.

The Commission will be independent of all ministries of the Government of India. It will have the autonomy to hire talent at various levels within and outside the government. It will also have the autonomy to define the compensation of its employees.

It is also crucial that NCHER develops a talented group of professionals who understand the proposed philosophy and see the difference between the existing and proposed processes.

It is important to keep in mind that the transition from the present regulatory system to the proposed one would not be easy. A smooth transition would require availing the expertise already available with the present apex bodies. Transition to the new organizational frame should enhance the people working in the present structures. Maximum care needs to be taken to ensure that the creation of the new apex body does not affect these people adversely. However, this need not be a constraint while deciding the structure of the new body. All this needs very careful analysis of the potential requirements. It is proposed that the job to provide operational frame should be assigned as a project on a consultancy basis to a competent professional organization. A task force would need to be constituted by the Government to work out the details of the process of implementation of the recommendations once they are accepted.

8

Grading System

INTRODUCTION

It is generally accepted that the concept of grading student's work quantitatively was developed by a tutor named William Farish and first implemented by the University of Cambridge in 1792. It is of interest to note that in India even after five decades, the grading system has been accepted only partially. It was the Secondary Education Commission (1952-53) appointed by the Government of India that mooted the idea of grading system.

SECONDARY EDUCATION COMMISSION ON THE GRADING SYSTEM

The Secondary Education Commission 1952-53, discussed the issue of examination and evaluation in Chapter XI of its report. It observed, "The present system of evaluating by percentiles *i.e.*, numerical marks, out of a hundred, may have certain advantages but the disadvantages seem to outweigh the advantages." The Commission pointed out the following demerits of the system of numerical marking system:

First, it introduces too many sub-divisions which are not only useless but cumbersome.

Secondly, it is indeed difficult to distinguish between two pupils one of whom obtains, say, 45 marks and another 46 to 47.

The Commission recommended the following grading system:

'A' to indicate 'Distinction'.

'B' to indicate 'Credit'.

'C' to indicate 'Pass'.

'D' and 'E' to indicate 'Failure' or 'Cases Referred Back'.

The Commission observed that the values of the categories in terms of percentile marks may be determined by the examining authority. Individual examiners in different subjects may even use percentile system and then convert the percentile scores in terms of categories.

The Commission was emphatic that this system would work in all cases except where the distinctions are to be made for the award of scholarships and prizes.

It appears the Commission was not very clear on this issue. Its recommendations do not seem to provide the appropriate solution.

'A MONOGRAPH ON GRADING IN UNIVERSITIES' (1976)

The Monograph published by the UGC gives the following demerits of numerical marking:

1. The standards of examiners differ very widely. There is a standard error of marking ranging from 5 to 20 marks in different subject.
2. Examiners have a tendency to give an unusually great number of 35 marks (when 35 is passing mark).
3. Examiners in different subjects use different ranges. In some the full scale of 0 to 100 is used, while in many other subjects, scales used are all different.
4. Marks given by examiners are not scaled.
5. Marks in different subjects are added up when they should not be.

OBJECTIVES OF THE GRADING SYSTEM

According to the '*Monograph*', grading system fulfills the following objectives:

(a) Evaluation which is mainly judgement based on measurement is uniform if all the universities agree to adopt the 7 point scale grading system.
(b) Comparability amongst various disciplines and within various subjects in a particular discipline is possible with the grading system.
(c) In case of grading system in all universities and boards, students can move from one university or board to another.
(d) Grading system takes the emphasis away from marks.

GRADES RECOMMENDED

Following grades were recommended for all subjects:

O	Outstanding	3%
A	Very Good	7%
B	Good	22%
C	Average	36%
D	Below Average	22%
E	Poor	7%
F	Very Poor	3%

DEMERITS OF THE GRADING SYSTEM

Prof. Atma Ram in '*Shikshak Salhi*' (May 2000) finds fault with the grading system on account of the following:

(i) It does not suit a selection situation. In view of the prevailing corruption, it can create chaotic conditions.
(ii) As the grading system does not allow ranking of the candidates, medals and prizes cannot be awarded to the deserving students.
(iii) The various appointing authorities want grades to be translated into percentage of marks.
(iv) Some education institutions are superior to others, in which case, grading of their students will not be comparable with those of others.

(v) In the grading system, there is little zeal or competition among students to strive for higher percentage of marks.

(vi) The Federation of Parents' Association, Delhi and the Delhi School Education Advisory Board, have stoutly opposed the move. They have termed it as a ploy of the NCERT to hide inefficiency. "When it (CBSE) should have worked on the revaluation system, it has embarked on a scheme to get away with its sloppy evaluation system", said Mr. Vijender Kumar, President, Delhi Abhibhavak Maha Sangh.

(vii) Some view it as a method to raise the pass percentage of government schools, to equate them with those of public schools.

He has further observed, "In terms of pure theory and academic considerations, the grading system may sound effective and desirable, but it does not suit the socio-economic conditions prevalent in the country. That it works well in several advanced countries in the world is no reason to believe that it will succeed here as well. In India, the realities of life, at the grass-roots level particularly, are different. It is not for nothing that in decades, out of 242 universities in India, only a few have opted for the grade system. We do not stress adequately the areas where revamping should be done and only hit upon short cuts and cosmetic, measures to improve the system of education or examination. At the evaluation stage, the examining body has broad-based interaction with the society. It should, therefore, take into confidence various constituents of society—students, teachers, parents, NGOs and general public. What we essentially need in education is due stress on effective teaching—220 teaching days in schools."

CBSE TO INTRODUCE GRADING SYSTEM

CBSE Chairman Ashok Ganguli made the following announcements on September 21, 2005:

1. From the academic session 2007-2008, the term 'pass' or 'fail' will not be mentioned in the certificate of class X.
2. The report card will mention the GPA (Grade Point Average) score.
3. The topmost grade will have a numerical value of 9.
4. The system will start for class IX in the 2006-2007 academic session.
5. The question papers for science, mathematics and social sciences in the class X examination and those for physics, chemistry, mathematics, biology, accountancy, business studies and accountancy, in class XII will be so designed that an average student is able to complete the paper in two and half hours.
6. The examination time will remain three hours plus the 15 minutes "cooling off" time the board had earlier announced.
7. The relative weightage of the subjects will be determined as per local needs.
8. From 2007, students would be required to answer a 60-mark theory paper instead of the 75-mark paper.
9. The remaining 40 marks will be divided between internal assessment, viva voce, practical project and a 20-mark objective-type written paper based on practicals.
10. Students will be required to get qualifying grades in four subjects out of five in order to be promoted to class XI.

(*Source*: *Times of India*, September 22, 2005)

THE COUNCIL OF BOARDS OF SCHOOL EXAMINATION (COBSE) IN INDIA ON EXAMINATION REFORMS

The Council of Boards of School Education in India (COBSE), an apex body of 41 educational boards from across the country, has rejected the suggestion to do away with the Class X board examination stating that any dilution of the "existing system is uncalled for".

Officials belonging to 31 boards participated in a deliberative session to discuss the NCF 2005. Six states—J&K, Himachal Pradesh, Maharashtra, Karnataka, Tamil Nadu, Tripura—did not participate in the discussion. The body came up with a slew of suggestions, foremost among which are exam reforms:

- Paper duration between 2½ and 3 hours. 15 minutes cool-off time
- Question paper should contain long, short, very short answers and multiple choice questions to reduce length, but at the same time maintain quality
- Results be declared in grades, marks also allowed in transitional phase
- 20 per cent marks in board exams be set apart for school based assessment of scholastic and co-scholastic areas
- Career guidance, counselling units in all schools. Teachers be trained to do counselling
- No to two levels of courses and curricular level—said students need basic grounding in all subjects. Subjects like higher mathematics can be offered as additional subjects
- Compulsory math laboratory in all schools
- Science be taught as part of environmental studies from Class I to V.
- Class VI to VIII be taught as a separate subject
- For Class XI and X introduce single science syllabus including physics, chemistry, biology etc.

MIXED REACTION TO PROPOSALS

The changes will reduce stress among school children. For bright students, the extra 15 minutes will not mean much. But for the average performer, it time will be crucial.

Jyoti Bose, principal, Springdales, Dhaula Kuan

Each school wants to improve its results and teachers and the management will try to manipulate results of internal assessments. There will definitely be a decline in the standard of education.

P. Soni, Principal, Kendriya Vidyalaya, R.K. Puram

The extra 15 minutes is good. But stress cannot be relieved completely by only these measures. Schools need to do away with pre-boards. Boards shouldn't be hyped, too

Vithika Rahul, counsellor Birla Vidya Niketan

Source: *Hindustan Times*, September 22, 2005

9

Follow up Action on Continuous and Comprehensive Evaluation by Central Board of Secondary Education (CBSE) 2009

With a view to implements some of the reform initiated by the Human Resource Development Minster, the CBSE has introduced a scheme of continuous and comprehensive evaluation in class IX and X. For the guidance of the principals, teachers and others it has published 'Teachers' Manual on Continuous and Comprehensive evaluation for class IX and X'. Some relevant extracts from the document are given here.

CONTINUOUS AND COMPREHENSIVE EVALUATION

Education aims at making children capable of becoming responsible, productive and useful members of society. Knowledge skills and attitudes are built through learning experiences and opportunities created for learners in school. It is in the classroom that learners can analyse and evaluate their experiences, learn to doubt, to question to investigate and to think independently.

Globalisation in every sphere of society have important implications for education. We are witnessing the increasing commercialisation of education. We need to be vigilant about the pressures to commodify schools and the application of market-related concepts to schools and school quality. The increasingly competitive environment into which schools are being drawn and the aspirations of parents place a tremendous burden of stress and anxiety on children, including the very young to the detriment of their personal growth and development, and thus hamper the joy of learning.

The aims of education simultaneously reflect the current needs and aspirations of a society as well as its lasting values and the immediate concerns of a community as well as broad human ideals. At any given time and place they can be called the contemporary and contextual articulations of broad and lasting human aspirations and values.

An understanding of learners, educational aims, the nature of knowledge, and the nature of the school as a social space can help us arrive at principles to guide classroom practices. Conceptual development is thus a continuous process of deepening and enriching connections and acquiring new layers of meaning. Alongside is the development of theories that children have about the natural and social worlds, including themselves in relation to others, which provide them with explanations for why things are the way they are, the relationships between causes and effects, and the bases for decisions and acting. Attitudes, emotions and values are thus an integral part of cognitive development, and are linked to the development of language, mental representations, concepts and reasoning.

As children's metacognitive capabilities develop, they become more aware of their own beliefs and capable of regulating their own learning.

Characteristics of Learning

- All children are naturally motivated to learn and are capable of learning.
- Making meaning and developing the capacity for abstract thinking, reflection and work are the most important aspects of learning.
- Children learn in a variety of ways-through experience, making and doing things, experimentation, reading, discussion, asking, listening, thinking and reflecting, and expressing oneself in speech, movement or writing-both individually and with others. They require opportunities of all these kinds in the course of their development.
- Teaching something before the child is cognitively ready takes away from real learning. Children may *'remember'* many facts but they may not understand them or be able to relate them to the world around them.

(Contd.)

- Learning takes place both within school and outside school. Learning is enriched if the two arenas interact with each other. Art and work provide opportunities for holistic learning that is rich in tacit and aesthetic components. Such experiences are essential to be learnt through direct experience, and integrated into life.
- Learning must be paced so that it allows learners to engage with concepts and deepen understanding, rather than remembering only to forget after examinations. At the same time learning must provide variety and challenge, and be interesting and engaging. Boredom is a sign that the task may have become mechanically repetitive for the child and of little cognitive value.
- Learning can take place with or without mediation. In the case of the latter, the social context and interactions, especially with those who are capable, provide avenues for learners to work at cognitive levels above their own.

Examinations are an indispensable part of the educational process as some form of assessment is necessary to determine the effectiveness of teaching learning processes and their internalization by learners. Various Commissions and Committees have felt the need for examination reforms. The *Hunter Commission (1882), Calcutta University Commission or Sadler Commission (1917-1919), Hartog Committee Report (1929), the Report of Central Advisory Board/Sargent Plan (1944), Secondary Education Commission/Mudaliar Commission (1952-53)* have all made recommendations regarding reducing emphasis on external examination and encouraging internal assessment through Continuous and Comprehensive Evaluation.

This aspect has been strongly taken care of in the National Policy on Education-1986 which states that *"Continuous and Comprehensive Evaluation that incorporates both scholastic and non-scholastic aspects of evaluation, spread over the total span of instructional time"* {8.24 (iii)}.

Report on the Committee for Review of NPE-1986-recommendation brought out by Government of India in 1991 lays down norms for *"continuous comprehensive internal evaluation and suggests safeguards against abuse of this evaluation system"*{268(iv)}.

Report on the *CABE Committee on Policy* brought out by MHRD, Govt. of India in January, 1992 has also referred to the provisions of NPE with regard to evaluation process and examination reforms and also suggested *'continuous and comprehensive internal evaluation of the scholastic and non-scholastic achievement of the students'* (16.8).

The need for Continuous and Comprehensive School-based Evaluation has been reiterated over the last few decades. The *Kothari Commission report (1966)* observed, *'On the completion of the course, at the end of the lower or higher secondary stage, the student should receive a certificate from the school also giving the record of his internal assessment as contained in his cumulative record. This certificate may be attached to that given by the Board in connection with the external examination...' (9.81).* It further adds, *'This internal assessment or evaluation conducted by the schools is of greater significance and should be given increasing importance. It should be comprehensive, evaluating all those aspects of students' growth that are measured by the external examination and also those personality traits, interests and attitudes which cannot be assessed by it.'* (9.84).

The Report of the Task Force on the Role and status of the Board of Secondary Education (1997) observed: *In our scheme of things, it is the School Boards which are expected to play the central role in the academic renovation of the school system. In other words, leadership has to come from the Board.* Once the Boards get committed to this vital and supplementary system of evaluation and push it vigorously, this innovation will come to be accepted by more and more schools.

Remodelling of School Education Boards—a report on the Task Force on the role and the status of *Boards of Secondary Education (1997)* has explained the philosophy of CCE (4.39). It further states that *'no agency other than the Boards should promote CCE and that is why it is sought to be emphasized that the Boards have to play a pioneering role in this regard'*(4.40).

"Learning without Burden"—a Report of the National Advisory Committee appointed by the Ministry of Human Resource Development, Department of Education, Govt. of India has stated that:

"Board examination, taken at the end of Class X and XII, have remained rigid, bureaucratic, and essentially uneducative..."

Accordingly, National Curriculum Framework–2005 (NCF-05) proposing Examination Reforms stated—*"Indeed, boards should consider, as a long-term measure, making the Class X examination optional, thus permitting students continuing in the same school (and who do not need a board certificate) to take an internal school examination instead"*.

As a sequel to above, the Position Paper on *'Examination Reforms' by NCERT 2006, says,*

> *"Indeed, it is our view that the tenth grade exam be made optional forthwith. Tenth-graders who intend continuing in the eleventh grade at the same school and do not need the Board certificate for any immediate purpose, should be free to take a school-conducted exam instead of the Board exam."*

Evaluation is goal directed, and educational outcomes are judged in terms of goal attainment. Every educational programme should aim for the all round development of the personality of the child. Therefore, the learning experiences provided in the school should contribute toward the achievement of the desired goals. A teacher, while deciding about the related learning experience should see both scholastic and co-scholastic outcomes as desirable behavioural outcomes of that programme.

The scope of evaluation in schools extends to almost all the areas of learners' personality development. It should include both scholastic and co-scholastic areas, i.e. it should be *comprehensive* in nature. This is in line with the goals of education. Evaluation is continuous and reveals the strengths and weaknesses of learners more frequently, so that the learners have better opportunity to understand and improve themselves. It also provides feedback to the teachers for modifying their teaching strategies.

Obviously, the efforts of CBSE to provide a leadership and pioneering role in implementing CCE is a major breakthrough which attempts to elevate the status of the schools as equal partners of the Board in assessing the attainment levels of the learner for public consumption through a separate independent certificate issued by the schools under the directive of the Board.

PLACE OF EVALUATION IN THE CURRICULUM

A curriculum is what constitutes a total teaching-learning programme composed of overall aims, syllabus, materials, methods and assessment. In short it provides a framework of knowledge and capabilities, seen as appropriate to a particular level. The syllabus provides a statement of purpose, means and standards against which one can check the effectiveness of the programme and the progress made by the learners. Evaluation not only measures the progress and achievement of the learners but also the effectiveness of the teaching materials and methods used for transaction. Hence evaluation should be viewed as a component of curriculum with the twin purpose of effective delivery and further improvement in the teaching learning process.

Understood properly, evaluation or assessment will not be perceived as something administered by the teachers and taken by the learners on the conclusion of a period of learning. When evaluation is seen as an end of the learning exercise, both the teachers and the learners will tend to keep it outside the teaching-learning process, rendering assessment broadly irrelevant and alien to the curriculum. Further such a perception associates anxiety and stress with evaluation for learners. On the contrary, *if evaluation is seen as an integral part built into the teaching learning process; it will become continuous like both teaching and learning.* When evaluation is subsumed into teaching learning, learners will not perceive tests and examination with fear. CCE will lead to diagnosis, remediation and enhancement of learning.

EVALUATION RESULTS: FUNDAMENTAL TO EFFECTIVE TEACHING AND LEARNING

Success in education is determined by the extent to which the learning objectives are realized. The progress towards attainment of objectives has to be assessed and evaluated for otherwise, we will not know where we are going.

One of the main purposes of evaluation at the school stage is to help the learner's improve their achievement in scholastic areas and to develop Life Skills and attitudes with reference to the larger context and canvas of life.

Further, in NPE (1986) it has been emphasized that at the school level the evaluation should be formative or developmental in nature because at this stage child is in the formative stage of learning and thus the emphasis should be on improvement of learning.

What is 'Continuous' and 'Comprehensive' Evaluation?

Continuous and Comprehensive Evaluation (CCE) refers to a system of school-based evaluation of students that covers all aspects of students development.

It is a developmental process of assessment which emphasizes on two fold objectives. These objectives are continuity in evaluation and assessment of broad based learning and behavioural outcomes on the other.

In this scheme the term *'continuous'* is meant to emphasise that evaluation of identified aspects of students *'growth and development'* is a continuous process rather than an event, built into the total teaching-learning process and spread over the entire span of academic session. It means *regularity of assessment, frequency of unit testing, diagnosis of learning gaps, use of corrective measures, retesting* and *feedback of evidence to teachers and students* for their self evaluation.

The second term *'comprehensive'* means that the scheme attempts to cover both the scholastic and the co-scholastic aspects of students' growth and development. *Since abilities, attitudes and aptitudes can manifest themselves in forms other then the written word, the term refers to application of variety of tools and techniques (both testing and non-testing) and aims at assessing a learner's development in areas of learning like:*

- Knowledge

- Understanding/Comprehension
- Applying
- Analyzing
- Evaluating
- Creating

The scheme is thus a curricular initiative, attempting to shift emphasis from testing to holistic learning. It aims at creating good citizens possessing sound health, appropriate skills and desirable qualities besides academic excellence. It is hoped that this will equip the learners to meet the challenges of life with confidence and success.

The objectives of the Scheme are:

- To help develop cognitive, psychomotor and affective skills.
- To lay emphasis on thought process and de-emphasise memorization
- To make evaluation an integral part of teaching-learning process
- To use evaluation for improvement of students achievement and teaching-learning strategies on the basis of regular diagnosis followed by remedial instruction
- To use evaluation as a quality control devise to maintain desired standard of performance
- To determine social utility, desirability or effectiveness of a programme and take appropriate decisions about the learner, the process of learning and the learning environment
- To make the process of teaching and learning a learner-centered activity.

What should be Assessed?

Since education is concerned with the total all-round development of the child, *(physical, socio-emotional, intellectual etc)* all aspects of the child's development need to be assessed. At the moment we do not assess the whole child, but only his or her academic achievement in specific areas. We assess learner's basically on examination results, we do not assess effort, performance, attitudes to learning, ability to practically apply what is learned in every day situations, nor do we assess them on how creatively they use techniques or critically evaluate different theories.

To make the process more comprehensive in nature, it is important that assessment of the child's learning be done in a whole range of situations and environments both in and out of the classroom. The assessment process also needs to be part of the way of providing information and feedback on the extent to which the school and teachers have been successful in realizing the expected outcomes of education.

In view of getting a complete picture of the child's learning, assessment should focus on the learner's ability to:

- learn and acquire desired skills related to different subject areas
- acquire a level of achievement in different subject areas in the requisite measure
- develop child's individual skills, interests, attitudes and motivation
- understand and lead a healthy and a productive life.
- monitor the changes taking place in child's learning, behaviour and progress over time.
- respond to different situations and opportunities both in and out of school.
- apply what is learned in a variety of environments, circumstances and situations
- work independently, collaboratively and harmoniously
- analyze and evaluate
- be aware of social and environmental issues
- participate in social and environmental projects and causes
- retain what is learned over a period of time

Schools of the future will need to develop in their learners the ability to take risks, to be adaptable, to be flexible, to cope with constant change and become lifelong learners. In this context, learners become dynamic leaders with teachers as enablers.

Before looking at how assessment is to be undertaken teachers need to determine objectives for achievement at secondary level. They need to look at what Secondary Education should develop in children not only in cognitive domain but also psychomotor and affective domains. Along with those attributes mentioned above they need to incorporate different age related indices and behaviours into the assessment criteria and practices. They also need to determine what their expectations are from the learner at the end of the secondary stage, and what kind of profile report is required in relation to different aspects and learning areas, that reflect the child's rapidly changing, personal development.

Thus assessment is a useful, desirable and an enabling process. To realize this one needs to keep the following parameters in mind-

The need to:

- assess the learner.
- use a variety of ways to collect information about the learner's learning and progress in subjects and cross curricular boundaries.
- collect information continuously and record the same.
- give importance to each learner's way of responding and learning and time it takes to do so.
- report on an ongoing continuous basis and be sensitive to every learner's responses.
- provide feedback that will lead to positive action and help the learner to do better.

In the assessment process, one should be careful NOT to:

- label learners as slow, poor, intelligent etc.
- make comparisons between them.
- make negative statements.

When should Assessment be Done?

Closely related to what needs to be assessed is the critical question about the periodicity of a child's progress. Assessment of the outcomes of learning in holistic education is integral to the teaching-learning process. Each session on learning should involve three parts: *process of learning, applying what has been learned, and assessment of what has been learned*. This is one way learning and assessment can combine.

In order to have Continuous and Comprehensive evaluation, both scholastic and co-scholastic aspects need to be given due recognition. Such a holistic assessment requires maintaining an ongoing, changing and comprehensive profile for each learner that is honest, encouraging and discreet. While teachers daily reflect, plan and implement remedial strategies, the child's ability to retain and articulate what has been learned over a period of time also requires periodic assessment. These assessments can take many forms but all of them should be as comprehensive and discreet as possible. *Weekly, fortnightly,* or *quarterly* reviews (depending on the learning area), that do not openly compare one learner with another and are positive and constructive experiences are generally recommended to promote and enhance not just learning and retention among children but their soft skills as well.

In order to improve the teaching learning process, Assessment should be both *Formative* and *Summative Assessment.*

Formative and Summative Assessment

Formative assessment is a tool used by the teacher to continuously monitor student progress in a non threatening, supportive environment. It involves regular descriptive feedback, a chance for the student to reflect on the performance, take advice and improve upon it. It involves students' being an essential part of assessment from designing criteria to assessing self or peers. If used effectively it can improve student performance tremendously while raising the self esteem of the child and reducing the work load of the teacher.

Some of the main features of Formative Assessment are listed below:

- is diagnostic and remedial
- makes the provision for effective feedback
- provides the platform for the active involvement of students in their own learning.
- enables teachers to adjust teaching to take account of the results of assessment
- recognizes the profound influence assessment has on the motivation and self-esteem of students, both of which are crucial influences on learning

- recognizes the need for students to be able to assess themselves and understand how to improve
- builds on students' prior knowledge and experience in designing what is taught.
- incorporates varied learning styles into deciding how and what to teach.
- encourages students to understand the criteria that will be used to judge their work
- offers an opportunity to students to improve their work after feedback,
- helps students to support their peers, and expect to be supported by them.

Formative assessment is thus carried out during a course of instruction for providing continuous feedback to both the teachers and the learners for taking decisions regarding appropriate modifications in the transactional procedures and learning activities.

Summative assessment is carried out at the end of a course of learning. It measures or *'sums-up'* how much a student has learned from the course. It is usually a graded test, i.e., it is marked according to a scale or set of grades.

Assessment that is predominantly of summative nature will not by itself be able to yield a valid measure of the growth and development of the child. It, at best, certifies the level of achievement only at a given point of time. The paper pencil tests are basically a one-time mode of assessment and to exclusively rely on it to decide about the development of a child is not only unfair but also unscientific. Over emphasis on examination marks focusing on only scholastic aspects makes children assume that assessment is different from learning, resulting in the *'learn and forget'* syndrome. Besides encouraging unhealthy competition, the overemphasis on Summative Assessment system also produces enormous stress and anxiety among the learners. It is this that has led to the emergence of the concept of Continuous and Comprehensive School-Based Evaluation.

Features of Continuous and Comprehensive Evaluation

- The *'continuous'* aspect of CCE takes care of *'continual'* and *'periodicity'* aspect of evaluation.
- Continual means assessment of students in the beginning of instructions (placement evaluation) and assessment during the instructional process *(formative evaluation)* done informally using multiple techniques of evaluation.
- Periodicity means assessment of performance done frequently at the end of unit/term *(summative)*
- The *'comprehensive'* component of CCE takes care of assessment of all round development of the child's personality. It includes assessment in ***Scholastic as well as Co-Scholastic*** aspects of the pupil's growth.
- Scholastic aspects include curricular areas or subject specific areas, whereas co-scholastic aspects include Life Skills, Co-Curricular, attitudes, and values.
- Assessment in scholastic areas is done informally and formally using multiple techniques of evaluation continually and periodically. The diagnostic evaluation takes place at the end of unit/term test. The causes of poor performance in some units are diagnosed using diagnostic tests. These are followed up with appropriate interventions followed by retesting.
- Assessment in Co-Scholastic areas is done using multiple techniques on the basis of identified criteria, while assessment in Life Skills is done on the basis of Indicators of Assessment and checklists.

Source-Examination Reforms, NCERT

Scholastic and Co-scholastic domain

The desirable behaviour related to the learner's knowledge, understanding, application, evaluation, analysis, and creating in subjects and the ability to apply it in an unfamiliar situation are some of the objectives in scholastic domain.

The desirable behaviour related to learner's Life Skills, attitudes, interests, values, co-curricular activities and physical health are described as skills to be acquired in co-scholastic domain.

The process of assessing the students' progress in achieving objectives related to scholastic and co-scholastic domain is called comprehensive evaluation. It has been observed that usually the scholastic areas such as knowledge and understanding of the facts, concepts, principles etc. of a subject are assessed. The co-scholastic elements are either altogether excluded from the evaluation process or they are not given adequate attention. For making the evaluation comprehensive, the scholastic and co-scholastic both should be given importance. Simple and manageable means of assessment of co-scholastic aspects of growth must be included in a comprehensive evaluation scheme.

In National Policy on Education (NPE) document, 1986 and as modified in 1992 also it is mentioned that the scheme of evaluation should cover all learning experiences of scholastic subjects and non-scholastic areas.

Comprehensive evaluation would necessitate the use of a variety of techniques and tools. This will be so because different specific areas of learner's growth can be evaluated through certain special techniques.

Functions of Comprehensive and Continuous Evaluation

In the teaching-learning process, the evaluation is expected to take care of scholastic and co-scholastic aspects. If a child is weak in some area, diagnostic evaluation and remedial measures should be adopted.

Important functions of Continuous and Comprehensive Evaluation are as follows:

- It helps the teacher to organize effective teaching strategies.
- Continuous evaluation helps in regular assessment to the extent and degree of Learner's progress (ability and achievement with reference to specific scholastic and co-scholastic areas).
- Continuous evaluation serves to diagnose weaknesses and permits the teacher to ascertain an individual learner's strengths and weaknesses and her needs. It provides immediate feedback to the teacher, who can then decide whether a particular unit or concept needs re-teaching in the whole class or whether a few individuals are in need of remedial instruction.

(*Contd.*)

- By continuous evaluation, children can know their strengths and weaknesses. It provides the child a realistic self assessment of how she studies. It can motivate children to develop good study habits, to correct errors, and to direct their activities towards the achievement of desired goals. It helps a learner to determine the areas of instruction in which more emphasis is required.
- Continuous and comprehensive evaluation identifies areas of aptitude and interest. It helps in identifying changes in attitudes, and value systems.
- It helps in making decisions for the future, regarding choice of subjects, courses and careers.
- It provides information/reports on the progress of students in scholastic and co-scholastic areas and thus helps in predicting the future successes of the learner.

Continuous evaluation helps in bringing awareness of the achievement to the child, teachers and parents from time to time. They can look into the probable cause of the fall in achievement if any, and may take remedial measures of instruction in which more emphasis is required.

Many times, because of some personal reasons, family problems or adjustment problems, the children stage neglecting their studies, resulting in sudden fall in their achievement.

If the teacher, child and parents do not come to know about this sudden fall in the achievement and the neglect studies by the child continues for a longer period then it will result in poor achievement and a permanent deficiency in learning for the child.

The major emphasis of CCE is on the continuous growth of students ensuring their intellectual, emotional, physical, cultural and social development and therefore will not be merely limited to assessment of learner's scholastic attainments. It uses assessment as a means of motivating learners in further programmes to provide information for arranging feedback and follow up work to improve upon the learning in the classroom and to present a comprehensive picture of a learner's profile.

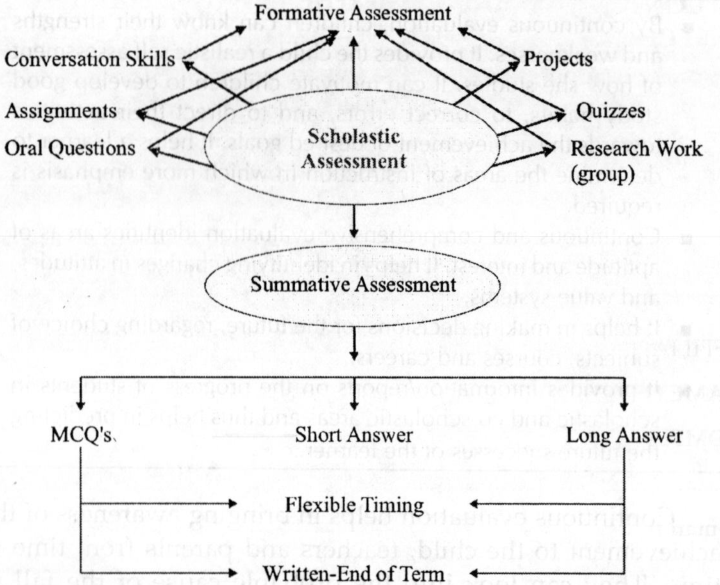
Formative Assessment
Conversation Skills
Projects
Assignments
Quizzes
Oral Questions
Scholastic Assessment
Research Work (group)
Summative Assessment
MCQ's
Short Answer
Long Answer
Flexible Timing
Written-End of Term

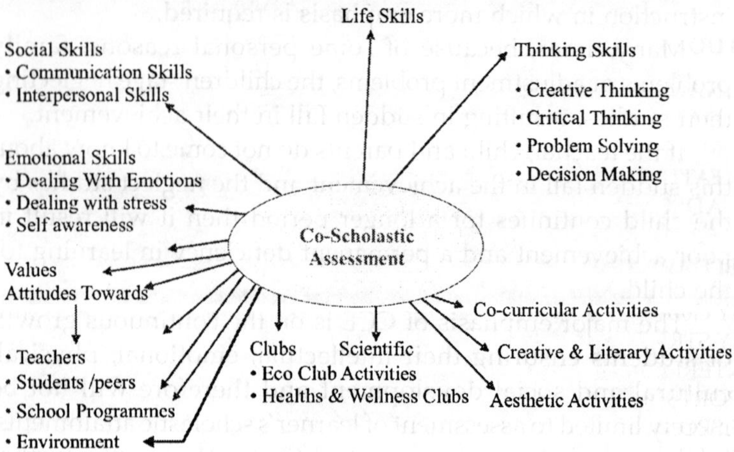
Life Skills
Social Skills
• Communication Skills
• Interpersonal Skills
Thinking Skills
• Creative Thinking
• Critical Thinking
• Problem Solving
• Decision Making
Emotional Skills
• Dealing With Emotions
• Dealing with stress
• Self awareness
Co-Scholastic Assessment
Values
Attitudes Towards
Co-curricular Activities
• Teachers
• Students /peers
• School Programmes
• Environment
Clubs
Scientific
• Eco Club Activities
• Healths & Wellness Clubs
Creative & Literary Activities
Aesthetic Activities

CONTINUOUS AND COMPREHENSIVE EVALUATION
CERTIFICATE OF SCHOOL—BASED ASSESSMENT

(Issued as per directives of
Central Board of Secondary Education, Delhi)

AFFILIATION NO. : ....

NAME OF SCHOOL : ....

COMPLETE ADDRESS : ....

....

E–mail Id : .... **Telephone No. :** ....

CLASSES IX–X
SESSION : 2009-2011

STUDENT PROFILE

1. NAME OF STUDENT : ____________		Student's Photo With Signature (Attested by the School Principal with School Seal)
2. DATE OF BIRTH : ____________		
3. MOTHER'S NAME : ____________		
4. FATHER'S NAME : ____________		
5. ADMISSION NO : ____________		

SELF AWARENESS

MY GOALS : ____________
MY STRENGTHS : ____________
INTERESTS & HOBBIES : ____________
SPORTS/GAMES : ____________
RESPONSIBILITIES DISCHARGED/
EXCEPTIONAL ACHIEVEMENTS :

____

____

Signature of Student | *Signature of Principal Seal* | *Signature of Board* | *Official Seal*

A. **PART—I : ACADEMIC PERFORMANCE : SCHOLASTIC AREAS**

Sl. No.	Subjects	Class IX				Class X			
		Formative Assessment	Summative Assessment	Overall Grade	Percentile Rank	Formative Assessment	Summative Assessment	Overall Grade	Percentile Rank
		Grade	Grade			Grade	Grade		
01	LANGUAGE-I								
02	LANGUAGE-II								
03	MATHEMATICS								
04	SCIENCE								
05	SOCIAL SCIENCE								
06*	I.T.								
07	H. Science								
08	Painting								
09	Music								
10	Book Keeping								
11*	Commerce/Accountancy								
12	Addl. Optional Subject								

* *Subjects listed from Serial No. 06 to 11 are prescribed by the CBSE for the children with Learning Disabilities.*

B.

Sl. No.		Class IX		Class X	
		Descriptive Indicators*	Overall Grade	Descriptive Indicators*	Overall Grade
1.	WORK EXPERIENCE				
2.	ART EDUCATION				
3.	PHYSICAL AND HEALTH EDUCATION/GAMES				

Attendance: Class IX
Total attendance of the student ....
Total working days ....

Attendance: Class X
Total attendance of the student ....
Total working days...............

PART 2: CO—SCHOLASTIC AREAS
2 (A): LIFE SKILLS

Sl. No.		Class IX		Class X	
	Life Skills	Descriptive Indicators*	Grade	Descriptive Indicators*	Grade
1.	Thinking Skills*				
2.	Social Skills*				
3.	Emotional Skills*				

* ***Thinking Skills*** *(Creative and Critical Thinking, Problem Solving, Decision Making, Self Awareness)*
Social Skills *(Interpersonal, Communication, Empathy) Emotional Skills (Coping with Stress, Coping with Emotions)*

* ***Descriptive Indicators are statements used to describe each learner. Suggestions are given in Teacher's Manual on School Based Assessment.***

2(B): ATTITUDES & VALUES
(Grading on a three point scale—A+, A & B)

S. No.		Class IX		Class X	
		Descriptive Indicators*	Grade	Descriptive Indicators*	Grade
1.	Attitude Towards				
1.1	Teachers				
1.2	School-mates				
1.3	School Programmes				
1.4	Environment				
2.	Value Systems				

LIFE SKILLS ASSESSMENT (2A)

***** The 5 point Grading Scale for Life Skills Assessment is given below:***

Most indicators in a skill - A+ Some indicators in a skill - B+
Many indicators in a skill - A Few indicators in a skill - B
Very few indicators in a skill - C

The Indicators of Assessment for each category of Life Skills are give below:

	Thinking Skills		**Social Skills**		**Emotional Skills**
	Student demonstrates the ability to:		***Student demonstrates the ability to:***		***Student demonstrates the ability to:***
1.	Be original, flexible and imaginative	1.	Identify, verbalize and respond effectively to other's emotions in an empathetic manner	1.	Identify one's own strengths and weaknesses
2.	Raise questions, identify and analyze problems	2.	Get along well with others	2.	Be comfortable with one's own self and overcome weaknesses for positive self-concept
3.	Implement a well thought out decision and take Responsibility	3.	Take criticism positively	3.	Identify causes and effects of stress one self
4.	Generate new ideas with fluency	4.	Listen actively	4.	Develop and use multi-faceted-strategies to deal with stress
5.	Elaborate/build on new ideas	5.	Communicate using appropriate words, intonation and body language	5.	Ability to express and respond to emotions with an awareness of the consequences.

* **The indicators for assessment of each category are given in Teachers' Manual for School Based Assessment.**

PART 3: CO-SCHOLASTIC ACTIVITIES

3(A): Literary & Creative Skills, Scientific Skills, Aesthetic Skills & Performing Art and Clubs

(Any two of the following to be assessed)

(Grading on a three point scale— A+, A & B)

Sl. No.	*Activities*	*Class IX*		*Class X*	
		*Descriptive Indicators**	*Grade*	*Descriptive Indicators**	*Grade*
01.	Literary & Creative Skills				
02.	Scientific Skills				

(*Contd.*)

03.	Aesthetic Skills and Performing Art				
04.	Clubs (Eco, Health and Wellness and others)				

Activities that can be used for:

Literary & Creative Skills : *Debate, Declamation, Creative Writing Recitation, Drawing, Poster—Making, Slogan Writing, On-the-Spot Painting, Theatre.*

Scientific Skills : *(Science Club, Projects, Maths Club, Science Quiz, Science Exhibition, Olympiads)*

Aesthetic Skills B *Music (Vocal, Instrument), Dance, Drama, Craft, Sculpture, Puppetry, Folk Art forms etc.*

3 (B) : HEALTH AND PHYSICAL EDUCATION
(Any two of the following to be assessed)
(Grading on a three point scale — A+, A & B)

1. Sports/Indigenous sports (Kho-Kho etc.)
2. NCC/NSS
3. Scouting and Guiding
4. Swimming
5. Gymnastics
6. Yoga
7. First Aid
8. Gardening/Shramdaan

S. No.		Class IX		Class X	
	Activity	Descriptive Indicators*	Grade	Descriptive Indicators*	Grade

Health Status

Height : .... Weight : ....

Blood Group: .... Vision : (L) ...., (R) ....

Teeth : .... Oral Hygiene: ....

Specific Ailment, if any: ....

....

Percentile—A percentile rank is the percentage of scores that fall below a given score. To find the percentile rank of a score x, out of a set of n scores, where x is not included, use.

$$\frac{\text{No.of score below}}{n} \times 100 = \text{Percentile Rank}$$

CONTINUOUS AND COMPREHENSIVE EVALUATION

1. Continuous and Comprehensive Evaluation is a process to provide holistic profile of the learner through regular assessment of both scholastic and co-scholastic aspects of development over the total span of learning time.
2. At it is spread over a period, of two years in classes IX & X, it provides several opportunities for the school to identify the latent talents of the learners in different domains.

GRADING SYSTEM

SCHOLASTIC A

MARKS RANGE	GRADE	GRADE POINT
91-100	A1	10.00
81-90	A2	9.0
71-80	B1	8.0
61-70	B2	7.0
51-60	C1	6.0
41-50	C2	5.0
33-40	D	4.0
21-32	E1	
00-20	E2	

SCHOLASTIC B

GRADE
A+
A
B+
B
C

Promotion is based on the day-to-day work of the students throughout the year and also on the performance in the terminal examination.

* First term – FA1 (10%) + FA2 (10%) + SA1 (20%)
  Formative Assessment (FA) 1 + 2 + 3 + 4 = 40%
* Second term – FA3 (10%) + FA4 (10%) + SA2 (40%)
  Summative Assessment (SA) 1+2 = 60%

10

Overview of Development and Recent Initiatives in Education

A. PRIMARY EDUCATION

The 86th Constitutional Amendment Act, 2002 led to insertion of a new Article 21-A in Part III of the Constitution that made Free and Compulsory Education to all children of 6 to 14 years of age a Fundamental Right. A suitable follow-up legislation to give effect to the 86th Constitution Amendment has been passed by the parliament in 2009. Important features of this legislation are taken up in the second part of this chapter.

The progress made in some of important primary education schemes is given below:

Sarva Shiksha Abhiyan

SSA is being implemented in partnership with State Governments to address the needs of children in age group of 6-14 years. The achievements of SSA till December 2008 are opening of 2,76,903 new schools, construction of 2,25,383 school buildings, construction of 9,18,981 additional classrooms, 1,82,019 drinking water facilities, construction of 2,51,023 toilets, supply of free textbooks to 8.40 crore children, appointment of 9.66 lakh teachers and in-service training for 23.82 lakh teachers. There has been a significant reduction in the number of out-of-school children on account of SSA interventions.

National Programme for Education of Girls at Elementary Education

NPEGEL is being implemented in educationally backward blocks (EBBs) where the level of rural female literacy is less than the national average and the gender gap is more than the national average and blocks having at least 5 per cent SC/ST population with SC/ST female literacy below 10 per cent. It is also being implemented in select urban slums. About 3,286 educationally backward blocks are covered under the scheme in 25 States. Under NPEGEL, 39,852 model schools have been opened in addition to supporting 11,261 Early Childhood Care and Education (ECCE) centres. Besides, 27,282 additional classrooms have been constructed, and 2,11,215 teachers have been given training on gender sensitization. Remedial teaching has also been provided to 11,44,370 girls apart from holding bridge courses covering 89,462 girls and additional incentives like uniforms etc. to about 1,60,73,048 girls till 31 January, 2009.

National Programme of Mid-Day Meals in Schools

The programme provides a mid-day meal of 450 calories and 12 grams of protein to children at the primary stage. For children at the upper primary stage, the nutritional value is fixed at 700 calories and 20 grams of protein. Adequate quantities of micro-nutrients like iron, folic acid and vitamin-A are also recommended under the programme. Since April 1,2008, it covers all children studying in government, local body and government-aided primary and upper primary schools and the Education Guarantee Scheme/Alternative and Innovative Education centres of all areas across the country. During 2008-09, 11.74 crore children were benefited under the scheme.

Kasturba Gandhi Balika Vidyalaya-KGBV

This Scheme was launched in July 2004 for setting up residential schools at upper primary level for girls belonging to predominantly to SC, ST. OBC and minority communities. The

KGBV scheme was merged with the Sarva Shiksha Abhiyan (SSA) as of April 1, 2007. 2,573 KGBVs were sanctioned by Government of India up to March 31, 2009. As on March 31, 2009, 2,460 KGBVs are reported to be functional (i.e. 95.61 per cent) in the States and 2,15,269 girls enrolled in them—53,503 SC girls (24.85 per cent); 74,487 ST girls (34.60 per cent); 54,201 OBC girls (25.18 per cent); 18,647 below poverty line (BPL) girls, (8.66 per cent), and 14,431 minority girls (6.7 per cent).

B. SECONDARY EDUCATION

Secondary education serves as a bridge between primary and higher education and prepares young persons between the age group of 14-18 years for entry into higher education and work. The number of secondary and higher secondary schools increased from 7,416 in 1950-51 to 1,68,900 in 2006-07. Total enrolment in secondary and higher secondary stage increased correspondingly from 1.5 million in 1950-51 to 39.44 million in 2006-07. Gross Enrolment Ratio (GER), which shows total enrolment in secondary stage (9th-12th) as a percentage of total population in the relevant age-group also increased steadily from 19.3 in 1990-91 to 40.62 in 2006-07. GER for Class IX-X (14-16 years) was 52.26 and for Class XI-XII (16-18 years) was 28.54 in 2006-07. Important Government initiatives for providing enhanced access to secondary education are:

- A comprehensive Centrally-sponsored scheme called Rashtriya Madhyamik Shiksha Abhiyan was launched in 2008-09 with the objective to universalize access and to improve quality of secondary education.
- Government of India has launched a Centrally-sponsored schemes called the National Means-cum-Merit Scholarship Scheme to award 1,00,000 scholarships each year, under which each student will be given Rs. 6,000 per annum (Rs. 500 per month) for study in Class IX to XII. To fund this scheme, a corpus of Rs. 750 crore already been created with the State Bank of India in 2008-09 and a like amount would be added

to this corpus fund every year over the next three years.

- First phase of a new Centrally-sponsored scheme to establish one high quality model school in each block of the country to serve as schools of excellence has been launched from 2008-09.
- The Government of India launched a Centrally-sponsored scheme called "Incentive to Girls for Secondary Education" in June 2008. According to the scheme, a sum of Rs. 3,000 will be deposited in the name of eligible girl as fixed deposit and she would be entitled to withdraw it along with interest thereon on reaching 18 years of age. The scheme will cover (i) All eligible girls belonging to SC/ST communities, who pass Class VIII and (ii) All girls who pass Class VIII examination from Kasturba Gandhi Balika Vidyalayas (irrespective of whether they belong to SC/ST) and enroll in Class IX in Government, Government-aided and local body schools.
- A new Centrally-sponsored scheme to set up girls hostels in about 3,500 educationally backward blocks was launched in 2008-09. Under this scheme, priority will be given to girls belonging to SC/ST/OBC/minority communities.
- Setting up of 20 Navodaya Vidyalayas which are residential schools meant primarily for meritorious rural children in districts having a large concentration of Scheduled Castes and Scheduled Tribes has been sanctioned.

C. HIGHER AND TECHNICAL EDUCATION

According to the University Grants Commission (UGC), enrolment in various courses at all levels in universities/colleges and other institutions of higher education in 2006-07 was 11.61 million as compared to 11.34 million in the previous year. Out of this, the number of women students were 4.70 million constituting 40.55 per cent. There has also been a significant expansion of Central institutions of higher education in recent years. Recent expansion of higher educational institutions includes the following:

- An ordinance has been promulgated under Article 123 of the Constitution for establishment of 15 Central Universities including the conversion of three State Universities into Central Universities—one in each such State which does not have a Central University, except Goa, which has not been included at the request of the State Government.
- Six new Indian Institutes of Technology (IITs), one each in Bihar, Andhra Pradesh, Rajasthan, Orissa, Gujarat and Punjab were set up during 2008-09. Classes were started from the academic session 2008-09.
- One new Indian Institute of Management (IIM), namely the Rajiv Gandhi Indian Institute of Management (RGIIM) at Shillong in Meghalaya, started functioning from the academic session 2008-09.
- Two new Indian Institutes of Science Education & Research (IISERs) set up at Bhopal and Thiruvananthapuram which have started functioning with the academic session 2008-09.
- Two new Schools of Planning & Architecture (SPAs) have been set up in Bhopal in Madhya Pradesh and Vijaywada in Andhra Pradesh. Classes started from the academic session 2008-09.
- One new Central University, namely Indira Gandhi National Tribal University at Amarkantak in Madhya Pradesh has started functioning.
- A new Scholarship Scheme has been started to cover top 2 per cent of the student population of Class XII (equally divided between boys and girls on the basis of Class XII results) by providing them with scholarship of Rs. 1,000 per month for 10 months in a year for the first three years of undergraduate level studies and Rs. 2,000 per month for 10 months in a year for subsequent 2 years.
- A "Submission on Polytechnics" has been launched,

wherein it is proposed to (i) assist the establishment of 1,000 new polytechnics by the State Governments throughout the country, (ii) provide assistance to 500 existing polytechnics to augment the facilities, (iii) provide assistance for construction of women's hostels in 500 polytechnic and (iv) start a renewed Community Polytechnic Scheme in 1,000 polytechnics in order to promote community development by providing short-term skill and vocational training to rural community and unorganized sectors.

- Central Institute of Classical Tamil has been set up and it has started functioning during 2008-09.
- To encourage research, the amount of fellowships under Junior Research Fellowships has been enhanced by about 50 per cent. The GATE qualified M.Tech Fellowship has also been enhanced from Rs. 5,000 per month to Rs. 8,000 per month.
- AICTE has permitted evening shits in the engineering college and polytechnics, subject to court directions in a New states.

REFORMS IN EDUCATION

Government policies have been focusing on providing quality education and upgrading skills. However, further reforms are needed in the education sector where both the Central and State Governments are involved (Box).

NEW INITIATIVES ANNOUNCED BY THE DEPARTMENT OF EDUCATION, HUMAN RESOURCE DEVELOPMENT MINISTRY, GOVERNMENT OF INDIA (HRDM)

On June 25, 2009, HRD Minister, Kapil Sibal rolled out a 100-day agenda which included the Following:

Schools Education

- Making class 10 board exam optional,

Box

Educational Reforms: Some Issues

Education in India comes under the concurrent list and thus both the Central and State Governments are involved leading to multiple controls and regulations by the governments and statutory bodies. There is an urgent need for replacement of bureaucratic controls in education by professional regulators along with private-public partnership to ensure universal primary education. Competition in tertiary and secondary education is also equally essential. Rating the quality of educational institutions and all education service providers (private and public) may be helpful. Entry of registered societies (non-profit) and publicly listed (education) companies n all fields of education, subject to the regulatory framework which ensures quality and reasonable pricing may be encouraged. Government's higher education funds should be focused on promoting scientific and technical education and encouraging R & D in all subjects. Education societies acquiring land at concessional rates or other assistance from the government should pass on the benefits to the students. There is a mad rush for higher education at prestigious institutions like IITs and IIMs. A large number of private coaching institutions are thriving on this phenomenon. Parents are incurring huge expenditure on their children to get coaching from the tutorial colleges to compete for engineering or management entrance examination. At the same time, there is heavy pressure on children which may adversely affect their physical and mental development. There is a need to streamline the admission procedure to such institutions while at the same time ensuring that quality of student intake does not suffer. Intake should be based on entrance examination which tests the aptitude to grasp knowledge and not the knowledge itself. Besides, the number of institutions could be increased through entry of private players while ensuring that they are professionally regulated so that their curriculum/degrees are internationally accepted.

Source: Adapted from '*Economic Survey*' 2008-2009 Govt. of India, New Delhi.

- Enactment of Right to Education Bill providing free and compulsory education to children 6 to 14 years,
- Public-Private Partnership (PPP) in school education,
- Evolving consensus for establishing All India Madrasa Board,
- Evolving National Curriculum Framework for Teacher Education,
- Replacing marks by grades for class 9 and 10 students in CBSE-affiliated schools,
- Establishment of an independent accreditation authority for schools,
- Recast adult Educat for the National Literacy Mission to focus on women.

There is also an attempt by the ministry to formulate a policy framework for public-private partnership (PPP) in school education by evolving a variety of PPP models and apply them as feasible. For instance, there could be private management of a badly-run municipal school besides inviting charitable institutions for imparting education.

Higher Education

Creation of a National Commission for Higher Education and Research (NCHER) for regulating higher education which will subsume in it agencies like the university grants commission (UGC), Medical Council of India (MCI) and the All India Council for Technical Education (AICTE).

- Reviewing the functioning of Deemed Universities.
- Making a law for mandatory assessment and accreditation of higher education institutions.
- Regulating entry and operation of foreign educational providers that will regulate these and let famous foreign universities enter India.

RIGHT TO EDUCATION BILL

The Lok Sabha passed the Right of Children to Free and Compulsory Education Bill 2009 on August 4, 2009.

The salient features of this Bill are:

- Children between 6 and 14 years are to be provided free and compulsory education.
- Schools must not fail kids up to Class VIII.
- Schools must admit children without school leaving certificates.
- Penalties for taking fees.
- Penalties for subjecting children or parents to screening procedures.
- Penalties for curriculum not being consistent with the Constitution of India.

- Penalties for ignoring social responsibility.
- Private schools to provide 25 percent seats to weaker sections.
- Teachers who are not adequately qualified have 5 years to acquire necessary qualifications.
- Inclusion of children who are disadvantaged because of disability.

APPENDIX II
EDUCATIONAL STATISTICS: EDUCATION IN INDIA VIS-À-VIS WORLD

Table: Number of Teachers by Types Schools, %age of Trained Teachers and Pupil Teacher Ratio and Pupil Teacher (2006-2007)

Type of Schools	*No. of Teachers (in lakh)*	*%age of Trained Teachers*	*Female Teachers per 100 Male Teachers*	*Pupil Teacher Ratio*
Primary	21.8	86	65	46
Upper Primary	16.7	87	67	34
High Schools	11.2	89	61	32
Hr./Sr. Secondary	10.3	80	62	34

Table: Gender Parity Index

(in %age)

Stages of Education	*Total*	*SC*	*ST*
Primary (I-V)	0.94	0.87	0.92
Upper Primary (VI-VIII)	0.88	0.80	0.84
Elementary (I-VIII)	0.92	0.86	0.90
Sec./Sr. Sec (IX-XII)	0.80	0.74	0.69
Higher Education	0.69	0.63	0.55

Gender Parity Index (GPI) is a ratio of Girls GER to Boys GER in a given level of education.

Source: Educational Statistics, Department of Education, NHRD.

Some Observations

A. Percentage of Trained Teachers

1. The percentage of trained teachers in Andhra Pradesh, Goa, Gujarat, Himachal Pradesh, Jharkhand, Karnataka, Kerala, Orissa, Tamil Nadu, Uttar Pradesh, Uttarakhand and Delhi is almost 100.
2. The percentage of trained teachers is less than 50 per cent in states: Arunachal Pradesh, Assam, Manipur, Meghalaya, Nagaland (21%) and Sikkim.

B. Pupil Teacher Ratio

Primary Stage:

Bihar	92
Haryana	57
Jharkhand	68
Uttar Pradesh	55
West Bengal	46
Orissa	0

Middle Stage:

Bihar	64
Haryana	60
Jharkhand	35
Uttar Pradesh	50
West Bengal	42
Orissa	36

High School:

1. Bihar	60
2. Jharkhand	53
3. Uttar Pradesh	60
4. West Bengal	55

Higher Secondary Schools:

1. Gujarat	38
2. Karnataka	80
3. Maharashtra	42

4. Uttar Pradesh 44
5. West Bengal 55

Education in India vis-à-vis World: Key Educational Parameters

The Table covers the following parameters:

1. Gross Enrolment Ratio at different stages
2. Literacy
3. Public Expenditure on Education

Table: International Comparison on Certain Other Key Educational Parameters-2005

Countries	*Gross Enrolment Ratio*				*Literacy*	*Public Exp. On Edu. As Percentage of GDP*
	Primary	*Lower Secondary*	*Upper Secondary*	*Tertiary*		
Countries with High EDI)>0.950)						
USA	99	102	88	83	n.a.	5.6
UK	107	103	107	60	n.a.	5.4
France	111	115	117	56	n.a.	5.9
German	101	102	96	n.a.	n.a.	4.6
Swedan	97	104	102	82	n.a.	7.4
Norway	98	102	127	80	n.a.	7.7
Countries with Medium EDI (0.800 to 0.950)						
Brazil	140	114	94	24	89	4.4
Mexico	109	104	55	24	92	5.4
China	113	101	50	20	91	n.a.
Egypt	101	96	75	34	71	n.a.
Indonesia	117	77	50	17	90	0.9
Sri Lanka	98	95	70	n.a.	91	n.a.
Countries with Low EDI (<0.800)						
Saudi Arabia	91	87	88	28	83	6.8
India	119	75	43	11	61	3.8
Pakistan	87	33	11	5	50	2.3
Bangladesh	109	64	34	6	47	2.5
Nigeria	103	37	31	10	69	n.a.

Source: Global Education Digest-2007 by UNESCO.

11

Essential Points Relating to Education Reforms and Implementation of the Act in the Present Scenario

Here a brief but meaningful effort is made to list a few essential points which need to be taken into consideration while planning and implementing educational reforms.

1. As far as possible exact estimates of financial resources should be made.
2. In the light of above suitable educational targets should be fixed.
3. For about 5 years there should be no talk of reforming education; instead every effort should be made to provide the required teachers for imparting education.
4. Adequate infrastructure should be made available in schools.
5. Sufficient 'teaching-learning' material should be provided to the institutions.
6. Since Central Board of secondary education(CBSE) and other 40 odd education / exam boards are usually vigilant to incorporate the latest technology and material in the curriculum, National and state educational organizations and institutions should keep their hands off.
7. Command, control and management of education should be in the hands of educators i.e. practioners (personnel belonging to IES (Indian Education Service and Provincial Education Service (PES). IAS and PCS services should not have any role in educational policy making and implementation.

8. The Department of Education and the Boards should fully collaborate in carrying out the needed reforms.
9. For the implementation of the Right to Education Act, no additional department/ post should be created. For the time being the entire staff of the National and state level educational organizations and institutions should be deputed to perform all relevant functions.
10. No Financial or other grant or support should be given to research organizations in the field of education.
11. For the time being no assistance/subsidy/grant should be provided to Non Governmental Organizations (which in most cases work on paper) for the promotion of Democracy, Secularism, Value Education, Population education, Environmental Education, etc. It has been reported in the newspapers from time to time that thousands of NGOs working in the field of adult education/adult literacy and social education have been blacklisted on account of their malpractices.
12. There should be no seminar, workshop etc. for about 5 years.
13. At the earliest delinking of degrees for jobs should be made.
14. Teacher pupil ratio at different levels of education should be maintained, i.e., Elementary -1:20, Secondary-1:30 and higher education 1:40.
15. Each teacher whether in college or in the university department should have 30 instructional hours per week.
16. Research work should be de-linked from educational duties. If a teacher is interested in guiding students he/she should do it during his/her spare time.
17. It is generally observed that thousands of research papers which are published in India have little relevance to the grass roots level situation. It is sheer waste of energy and money. A perusal of the research work done in India since 1960 indicates that no reform in education is based on research papers.

18. There should be no need to establish a number of universities as suggested by the High Level Committee. Instead our effort should be to strengthen the existing set-up and institutions and not to replace them. An example is given that in UK, there is a high powered special board to control and manage higher education. In this context we should not forget that India can accommodate 18 UKs, therefore in India the constitution of one regulatory higher authority may not be an appropriate step. Besides it must be remembered that education is a concurrent subject in the constitution and the views of the State Governments must be taken into account while taking decisions on such vital issues.

Summing up

The most important point is that every educational institution should be provided with adequate staff, infrastructure and teaching-material before launching any new reform/scheme and it should be ensured that the teachers teach and the students learn.

